Food Service Management

FOOD SERVICE MANAGEMENT

Harish Bhatt

CRESCENT
PUBLISHING CORPORATION

[*The responsibility for the facts stated, conclusions reached and plagiarism, if any, in this book is entirely that of the Author. And the Publisher bears no responsibility for them, whatsoever.*]

Food Service Management

First Published : 2006

ISBN 81-8342-002-8

Published by :

CRESCENT PUBLISHING CORPORATION
4831/24, Prahlad Street,
Ansari Road, Darya Ganj,
New Delhi - 110002
Ph. : 23272541, 23257835
Fax : 91- 011- 23257835
e-mail : campusbooks@hotmail.com

Typesetting by :

Arjun Computers
Delhi - 110051

Printed at :

S.P. Printech
Delhi

Preface

Food service management emphasizes acquiring those skills that are necessary to operate any type of food service activity and prepares our students to begin their careers at the managerial level. Food service managers have to perform variety of administrative assignments, such as keeping employee work records, preparing the payroll, and completing paperwork to comply with licensing laws and reporting requirements of tax, wage and hour, unemployment compensation, and social security laws.

This book intents to serve as a communication tool enabling students to develop confidence in their food service management skills by better preparing them for a successful management experience while also preparing them for the rigorous work of food service management. The major issues of food service management including service industry issues, consumer behaviour, workforce problems, marketplace diversity, growth strategies, professional development, legal and leadership issues etc., are described elaborately. For technical personnel, managers, and marketers in the food industry, it discusses the market and the players, new product technologies, product safety and microbiological technologies, and commercialization strategies.

Harish Bhatt

Contents

	Preface	*v*
1.	Basics of Catering Management	1
2.	Managing Food and Beverage Operations	45
3.	Management Priorities	76
4.	Food Processing	132
5.	Food Safety	212
6.	Organisational and Workforce Challenges	240
	Bibliography	280
	Index	282

1 Basics of Catering Management

Most common catering operations, are those that are readily identifiable as private rooms in restaurant operations, hotel facilities, and independent catering facilities. The increased demand by the international public for private function space outside of their own homes and businesses has led the catering segment of the foodservice sector of the hospitality industry to be a leader in the continued growth of both facilities and revenue. Forward thinking foodservice businesses from fine dining restaurants to delicatessens are incorporating catering services into their operations in recognition of the expanding market for prepared foodservices.

Foodservice operation refer to the opportunities management makes available to the customer to purchase food, beverage, entertainment, and ancillary services. Services include:

— Table foodservices

— Packaged take-out foodservices

— Beverage services

— Entertainment services

— Business meeting services
— Conference and convention services
— Contract feeding services
— Off-premise foodservices
— Home-replacement foodservices

Full-Service Restaurants

Full-service restaurants have the opportunity to offer a variety of catering services to their customers. Before any decision is made to offer these services, however, six important factors should be considered:

— Location
— Customer profile
— Restaurant style or concept
— Staffing capabilities
— Restaurant physical layout
— Cuisine and menu offerings

Location: The proximity of the restaurant to office complexes and centralized business areas will help to establish whether its catering service will be focused on business or social marketing efforts. Businesses in the twenty-first century are spread from urban centres to suburban locations in office parks. Central urban locations offer a concentrated market for both office delivery and take-out.

A significant factor in developing the market for business catering is that service is generally required during the business week, leaving weekend periods free to service social business. In addition, locations such as museums, concert halls, and historical sites offer interesting venues to catered functions for both local businesses and conventions.

Both urban and suburban restaurants can successfully develop social catering business. Suburban locations are generally more appropriate for social catering to private homes, clubs, churches, and other facilities. Delivery to urban locations can pose security and logistical problems, creating additional costs for transportation and service labour. Population density also affects the volume of anticipated catering business.

Restaurants situated in rural areas with low population density cannot expect immediate high volumes of catering business. Areas of high-density population yield a variety of catering opportunities that steadily increase in volume through referrals and reputation. The location of the physical restaurant building plays a role in the type of catering services to be offered. Storage facilities, expansion possibilities, and access to major transportation routes are factors important to catering service production.

Customer Profile: Restaurants have the advantage of a built-in customer pool to whom they can market in-house and off-premise catering services. In addition, the attraction of being associated with a restaurant's reputation will help to expand the possible market to include new business and social clients. The market profile should classify customers as business or social catering clients, designated by income bracket. In addition the range of activities for which each customer pool will need catering services should be researched as thoroughly as possible. This will help in developing package programs along with potential menu programs and accompanying pricing concepts.

Style or Concept: The style, concept, and/or theme of the restaurant should be taken into consideration when planning potential catering services. Off-premise catering services do not necessarily have to blend with the facilities offered by the restaurant. On-premise catering services should, however, be designed to function within the restaurant facilities.

Restaurants facilities: Restaurants facilities are a major factor in providing on-premise catering. The ratio of catering functions to restaurant services that can be handled at a given time is dependent on the size and flexibility of the physical plant. Small private parties are often incorporated into the general dining room setting. Large parties must, however, be given facilities that are separated from the general public.

Many restaurants that offer in-house catering schedule large parties, such as weddings, anniversaries, luncheons, and dinners, on days and times when the restaurant is not otherwise open. When management is continually turning away catering business, a decision will need to be made as to how the restaurant will balance is future development of catering versus full-service dining services. Kitchen facilities play a major part in determining when and how catering service demands can be met.

Kitchen equipment must be flexible, allowing for volume production to take place simultaneously with a la carte restaurant service. The kitchen cooking load and holding capacity of ovens and auxiliary equipment is important to determine if a kitchen is to be used to its full capacity during busy times. Storage and refrigeration facilities determine the amount of food products available at any given time. The cost of waste from food spoilage due to lack of refrigeration and freezer space could dilute the profit from additional catering business.

Take-out service is the most profitable way for restaurants and catering services to increase revenues without increasing costs. Because take-out service does not require extra seating, it generally will not require an operation to expand its facilities beyond accommodating takeout customers with a pickup and waiting area. Kitchen production can plan and schedule to handle large increases in volume for short time periods. In addition, take-out does not require the additional expenses incurred by table service for glassware, linens, flowers, menus, and entertainment. Disposable dishes, plastic flatware, and a carrying container are the basic requirements for take-out service.

Successful take-out service does, however, require planning to assure that customers receive menu items in satisfactory condition. As with the catering menu, the selection of take-out menu items should be drawn from the restaurant menu in order to maximize purchasing and production efforts.

The hotel food and beverage department provides food-related guest services throughout a hotel, conference, or resort property. Outlets for food and beverage services can include the following:

1. Full-service restaurant
2. Coffee shop
3. Catering facilities
4. Room service
5. Recreational areas
6. Lobby area bars
7. Food market or delicatessen

Food items for these combined foodservice areas are provided from a central kitchen, with the exception of large hotel facilities where satellite kitchens provide auxiliary production and service areas. An executive chef supervises production for all areas, consulting with the manager of each foodservice area. Of the seven food service areas, catering affords the possibility for the greatest profit, in addition to providing much-needed cash flow during periods when room sales are slow. Hotel catering services are usually classified as:

1. Business
2. Convention/conference
3. Social

The primary catering market for a hotel is based on three factors:

1. Location
2. Hotel facilities
3. Customer profile

Location: The location of a hotel determines the demand for in-house catering. In-house catering is defined as guest-related foodservice functions associated with business meetings, conferences, conventions, and social concerns. A hotel with a remote location focuses its catering efforts on the business booked into the hotel. Resort locations often provide additional opportunities for catering services at sports facilities and landscape venues throughout the property.

A hotel with a suburban or downtown location can expect to develop a large volume of outside catering business, both business-related and social in addition to conferences and conventions. The amount of combined catering business that can be handled at any one time in a hotel is based primarily on the number and size of the facilities available. The major function rooms are usually referred to as the ballroom areas. These are complemented by a series of meeting rooms, some adjacent to the main ballroom area and some located in other areas of the hotel.

The customer profile for hotel catering services is made up of both business and social clientele. Customers who use the hotel as a location for a two-or three-day meeting consider meal functions as part of the total meeting package. This arrangement not only enables customers to work within a budget that covers the entire project, but also fits with an approach to planning catering functions that considers the success of the overall meeting rather than each individual function.

The catering manager is generally given the responsibility of creating a menu plan for the entire program along with theme functions and special events. The target market for hotel catering functions is a customer who reflects the social, business, and economic profile of the community. Hotel catering services attract a wide base of customers with a broad range of requests.

Customers who plan business functions on a regular basis are familiar with the catering staff and services of the hotel. Their needs are often quickly identified and provided for. Customers who plan social functions on a one-time basis, however, need more personal guidance throughout much of the planning stage. Pricing is a primary concern of this customer group.

A catering hall is a facility dedicated to private parties with an on-site prediction kitchen and staff. These facilities can offer a wide range of both in-house and off-premise catering services. The major factors that influence the market for a catering hall are:

1. Style or concept
2. Facilities
3. Customer profile

Catering halls offer customers a self-contained private function space independent of a hotel or restaurant. Many catering halls specialize in social functions such as weddings and plan the design of the landscaping and building to accent such functions. This design is also often aimed at a particular segment of the customer market, depending on location of the hall and the density and ethnic background of the surrounding population.

Catering halls can also specialize in large functions, providing space for groups that cannot normally be accommodated in other facilities. Such halls are generally designed to host a wide range of social and business functions and a variety of special event themes.

The flexibility, and often the originality, of function spaces are important to the success of a catering hall. Customers will travel considerable distances to social functions held in facilities that offer a unique setting or experience. Wedding receptions are often planned in locations over an hour away from the site of the ceremony so that the bride and groom can have a specific setting for their reception. Catering halls can provide the setting for special event themes ranging from futuristic to country western, offering menu and entertainment packages to match.

The customer target market for catering halls, like hotels, is based on the social, business, and economic profile of the community. Catering halls, also like hotels, are available in a variety of price venues, generally appealing to customers who are looking for menu and function packages within a specific range of prices. Identifying a customer group toward which to target marketing efforts includes surveying the competition, establishing a price range, and determining specific geographic areas of the community in which potential customers live based on demographic information such as annual income, family size, and age.

Independent caterers are private businesses offering catering services to the general public. These businesses operate with or without permanent facilities of their own in which to hold functions. Those caterers who operate with-out a formal facility must arrange for kitchen production and storage space. Kitchen space can be rented from schools, churches, senior citizen centres, and other institutional facilities with commercial refrigeration and production space.

Storage space can be arranged for in self-storage warehouse rental facilities that combine short-term leases with flexible storage space and 24-hour access. Some catering companies have their own production facilities and enough warehouse space to handle large volumes of business. Chairs, floor covering, tables, and the table setup necessary for large functions are either sourced from a catering company's own warehouse or contracted through a local rental supplier.

Many independent caterers focus on off-premise catering, maintaining only a small catering hall with limited facilities to house their production and storage needs. Their focus is on both business and social functions within a wide geographical area. In order to successfully cater to as many functions as possible simultaneously, a catering company has to be extremely well organized. Although equipment needs, staffing, and transportation are major concerns, the primary product, food, is the most important issue.

The key to successfully providing catering services to a number of functions simultaneously is the duplication of as many of the menu items as possible in order to minimize kitchen production. All surrounding items, salads, and desserts can be standardized. The main course selection should be limited to three or four items on any given day if possible. Menu items should be chosen for their ability to be precooked for completion in another location.

Private clubs offer a self-contained facility that operates both full-service dining rooms and private function space along with a variety of food and beverage outlets. Private clubs are generally dependent on their membership for both dining room and catering business. Functioning as nonprofit organizations, clubs are, in many areas, prohibited by law from accepting or soliciting business from nonmembers. If such is the case private clubs may, however, cater functions that are sponsored by members and attended by nonmembers, allowing them to service both social and business activities.

Factors that influence the success of restaurant and hotel catering services, such as location, facilities, and customer profile, also affect private clubs. Off-premise catering services can also be offered to private club members. Private clubs may also contract out their foodservice operation to a contract foodservice operator. Club facilities can greatly influence the volume of catering business. Clubs offering spectacular settings, access to garden areas for outdoor functions, or well designed interiors, will easily attract social business.

Contract feeding companies provide institutions such as hospitals and schools, as well as businesses, with in-house meal programs designed to meet specific needs. Food production and service is contracted for long-term periods with designated budget restrictions. As food costs have increased and available labour decreased, institutions and businesses have turned to outside contractors to operate their food-service programs. In most cases, these programs function as a service to either patients, clients, or employees; they are subsidized benefits, not profit making operations. By using a professional contract foodservice operator to handle this area of operations, businesses find that the quality of service increases significantly along with client and employee satisfaction.

Charcuteries and Delicatessens: Charcuteries are food stores that offer take-out foodservice along with gourmet food products. Many of these products are used as ingredients in the preparation of the food line. In some cases a small seating area will be offered for eat-in customers. The trend for home-replacement food is significant to this type of operation. When customers want something beyond fast food for a take-home meal, they turn to establishments that can provide meals that they would like to have prepared for themselves. Home-replacement food is being provided in a number of types of foodservice facilities, including upscale supermarkets.

This type of foodservice operation usually specializes in a regional or national cuisine. Menu items range from salads and sandwiches to fully prepared meals. The success of a charcuterie depends on two major factors: location and customer profile. Charcuteries should be located where the customer profile supports the level of cuisine offered. Pricing for this type of foodservice operation is generally higher than that of delicatessens and supermarket preprepared and packaged food items; hence it requires a customer base willing to pay for gourmet food products.

Smaller independent caterers often operate out of this type of retail outlet, using the facility for both production and storage in addition to a means of advertising and promotion. Delicatessens are food stores that provide a variety of food products and offer both eat-in and take-out food service. The location should be reasonably close to the targeted customer base. Menu item offerings range from sandwiches, salads, and pizza to preprepared meals-to-go. Take-out foodservice of preprepared foods is a major business segment for this type of foodservice operation.

The profile of customers for a charcuterie/delicatessen operation is drawn largely from the demographics of the population in the immediate area of the business. Primary customers can be identified as either employees of adjacent businesses or local area residents. A customer profile is determined for each of the two primary customer groups.

For example, the twice a week business customer, with an average check of five to six dollars, could be in the mid-20s to 40s age group and low to middle income bracket. The local resident profile, with an average check of twelve dollars or more two times a week, may be in the mid-30s to 50s age group, middle to upper income bracket. Further investigation may show that the business employee is a morning coffee and lunch customer while the local resident is an evening customer for home-replacement meals.

Classification of Catering

Generally, catering operations are classified into two categories:

a) On-premise catering

b) Off-premise catering

On-premise catering is catering for any function-banquet, reception, or event-that is held on the physical premises of the establishment or facility that is producing the function. On-premise catering differs from off-premise catering, whereby the function takes place in a re-mote location, such as a client's home, a park, an art gallery, or even a parking lot, and the staff, food, and decor must be transported to that location. Off-premise catering often involves producing food at a central kitchen, with delivery to and service provided at the client's location. Part or all of the production of food may be executed or finished at the event location.

At times, off-premise caterers must rely on generators for electricity, truck in potable water, devise a trash system, and otherwise "rough it." Although some hotels and restaurants offer off-premise catering, most do not "cater-out." A few of them, however, have entered the off premise catering market and are capable of providing offsite production and service. Exact statistics are not kept for these two functions, but it is estimated that on-premise catering accounts for about two thirds of all catering sales in the United States, with off-premise cater-ing accounting for the remaining third.

Catering, both on-premise and off-premise, is one of the fastest growing segments of the U.S. foodservice industry and has enjoyed success and expansion over the years. The National Restaurant Association (NRA) notes that catering and takeout sales will generate considerable growth in U.S. foodservice sales throughout the foreseeable future. Every day thousands of business and social groups get together for their members to enjoy each other's company and the variety of refreshments that are usually found at these gatherings. Groups generally prefer professionally prepared and served food and beverages. This allows hosts to concentrate on their personal, social, and business activities, simultaneously enjoying the events. And, as a bonus, they can leave the cleanup to someone else.

On-premise caterers-such as hotels, convention centers, and restaurants-usually have the advantage of offering many services under one roof. They can also provide sufficient space to house an entire event and plenty of parking. In general, each catered event has one host and one bill. Many localities have independent banquet halls, civic auditoriums, stadiums, arenas, ethnic social clubs, fraternal organizations, women's clubs, private city or country clubs, athletic clubs, hospitals, universities, libraries, executive dining rooms in office buildings or corporate headquarters, churches, recreation rooms in large apartment or condominium complexes, parks, museums, aquariums, and restaurants with banquet rooms. Some of these facilities are often more competitive than hotels, as they have more flexible price structures because of their lower overhead expenses. Some are public facilities and are tax-exempt.

A number of these facilities provide their own catering in-house, others are leased to and operated by contract foodservice companies that have exclusive contracts. Still others will rent their facilities to off-premise caterers. Another recent competitor for catering business has been the proliferation of takeout services. Some supermarkets and department stores have developed gourmet takeout, deli, and bakery facilities, and many can produce beautiful, reasonably priced buffet platters. More and more restaurants are heavily engaged in takeout business, particularly around the holidays.

However, if not properly monitored, a "cater-out" can disrupt the normal work flow and efficiency of a restaurant, damage morale, and skew ordering and purchasing routines. Off-premise functions can be a significant source of additional sales revenue and profits for those hotels and restaurants that have the necessary equipment and personnel to handle large off site catered affairs. However, unless the facility is set up to do this correctly, the work can be too distracting and the added expense may wipe out any incremental profits. For example, transporting perishable food requires proper trucking for food safety. A refrigerated truck or a great amount of ice must be used to maintain safe temperatures.

Staffing is also an issue. Hotel servers are accustomed to a division of labor and often are not pleased when they are asked to perform tasks off-site that are not required when they are working within the facility. In a hotel, servers do not set up equipment or do the cleaning, hauling, and other duties that are required at an off-premise site. There may also be union implications if job descriptions are violated.

Catering can also be classified as social catering and corporate (or business) catering. Social catering includes such events as weddings, bar and bat mitzvahs, high school reunions, birthday parties, and charity events. Business catering includes such events as association conventions and meetings, civic meetings, corporate sales or stockholder meetings, recognition banquets, product launches, educational training sessions, seller-buyer entertaining, service awards banquets, and entertaining in hospitality suites. The estimated 75 percent of all catering sales generated by business catering is due to the sheer volume of people served daily at meetings in hotels and convention centers, where meals for thousands are produced regularly.

The hotel caterer is only one of many types of caterers that seek to satisfy the public's catering needs. A hotel usually has the advantage in this competitive field because it can normally offer many services under one roof as well as sufficient space to house an entire event, thereby enticing the customer with a one-stop-shopping opportunity. An upscale hotel often provides a more glamorous and exciting location.

The hotel must realize, however, that other caterers abound in the industry, and even though they may be much smaller and unable to offer a smorgasbord of choices, they nevertheless eagerly court many of the same customers sought by hotel caterers. For instance, in some parts of the country there are independent banquet halls, convention facilities, and conference centers. Some of these properties are able to compete with hotels for the same customers because they have more flexible price structures owing to lower overhead expenses.

A hotel may have the advantage in some instances: If a client is able to buy out the entire facility, the hotel can offer a generous price reduction because of the sleeping room revenue derived from the group. Some restaurant operations have attached banquet rooms that can be used for several types of catered events. It is expensive to maintain a room that may be empty three or four nights per week, so the banquet room is often used as overflow restaurant dining space on busy nights.

A restaurant can book many small functions if it takes time to court this business. However, before going after this business, the catering executive must be careful to avoid those catered events that cannot be charged enough to cover all variable and fixed overhead costs associated with opening a function room. For instance, a restaurant that uses a section of its regular dining room to house a catered event will not incur significantly greater heating and cooling expenses; the dining room must be heated or cooled regardless of the number of guests expected.

A hotel, however, must consider the feasibility of opening a function room; if the room is opened, incremental heating and cooling expenses will be incurred, whereas if the room remains closed, these expenses are avoidable. In some cases, although a particular group may turn a profit for the average restaurant, a hotel property may be less fortunate. Private clubs do a great deal of catering for their members. Country clubs concentrate on social events, such as weddings and dances. City clubs specialize in business catering, such as for corporate meetings, board luncheons, and civic events. Resorts often have outdoor functions at remote locations on the property.

Profitoriented hospitals do a good amount of catering business for medical meetings and staff functions. In most cases, they compete directly with hotels for these functions. There are several types of tax-exempt organizations that offer catering services to anyone willing to pay for them. For instance, universities, colleges, hospitals, libraries, churches, museums, and military clubs vigorously compete for catering events because they help subsidize their major nonprofit activities.

Many taxpaying catering businesses are especially unhappy with these so-called nonprofit competitors; however, nonprofit groups consistently fight any type of government restraints on these activities. Contract foodservice companies operate many facilities that are capable of supporting catering events. For instance, many of these firms operate foodservices in large office buildings, where executive dining rooms can be used to house special parties and meetings.

Some contract foodservice companies are also capable of handling off-premise catering functions. Most convention centers are public institutions that use in-house contract services typically operated by national catering companies. Privately owned companies function as an internal catering department and enjoy all of the amenities and unique environments offered by the facility. They tend to focus on conventions and trade shows and often have the opportunity to cater megaevents because of the large amount of exhibit space, as well as attached areas, available.

Some mobile caterers, with the proper equipment, provide complete meal production and service on location. For instance, a few companies specialize in feeding forest fire fighters, disaster relief workers, movie and television production crews in the field, people taking extended camping trips or fishing/rafting excursions, construction site workers, or other such groups.

Management Functions of Catering Service

The person in charge of the catering department must perform the normal management functions. He or she has the following responsibilities:

— *Planning:* The catering department must accomplish both financial and nonfinancial objectives. To do so, it must develop appropriate marketing, production, and service procedures. It must also ensure that the department's operating budgets and action plans are consistent with the facility's overall company objectives.

— *Organizing*: The catering department must organize the human and other resources needed to follow the plan.

Staff members must be recruited and trained. Work schedules must be prepared. And performance evaluations must be administered.

— *Directing*: Employee supervision is an integral part of every supervisor's job. The supervisory style will emanate from top management. The catering department's supervisory procedures must be consistent with company policies.

— *Controlling*: The catering department manager must ensure that actual performance corresponds with planned performance. Effective financial controls ensure that actual profit and loss statements are consistent with pro forma budgets, and effective quality controls ensure that production and service meet company standards.

Catering departments have a variety of objectives. The weight and priority given to each will depend on company off-premise cateringpolicy. The following are among the most common objectives:

— *Earn a fair profit on assets invested in the catering business.*

— *Generate sufficient catering sales volume, enough to defray all expenses and leave a fair profit*. Caterers must be careful not to generate a lot of business that will not pay for itself. They must practice selective sales strategies in order to maximize profits. Usually, the only time a catering executive should consider booking a marginally profitable event is if it is a party designed to show off the catering facilities, such as a charity event. It may also be contemplated if the property wants to host VIPs who may indirectly generate future catering revenues, or during the slow season, to keep staff employed.

— *Deliver customer satisfaction*. Meeting this objective will lead to repeat patronage as well as positive referrals. All foodservice operations, including the catering segment, thrive on repeat patronage.

— *Provide consistent quality and service*. Customers are happy when the actual quality and service received parallel those that were promised. Punctuality and consistency are hallmarks of a well-run catering department.

— *Convey a particular image*. Caterers often want to be known as specializing in certain types of products and services, such as weddings or unusual themed events. They strive to be unique because they want customers to think of them whenever a specific atmosphere or ambiance is required. Catering is often a facility's most visible characteristic on the local and national levels. It alone has the greatest potential to become a facility's "signature"-its major claim to fame.

— *Develop a reputation for dependability*. Regardless of the pressure that any event places on the staff, catering departments want clients to have confidence that their needs will be met. The catering department must adequately fill the role of liaison between clients and all of the property's services.

— *Develop a reputation for flexibility*. To be dependable, the caterer must be flexible. The catering department must be able to react on a moment's notice. Clients will remember fondly the facility that bailed them out at the last minute.

— *Stay on budget*. To meet this objective, the caterer must be on guard against adding "surprise" charges that go over budget.

Catering departments are organized according to the needs of the particular facility. For example, a hotel's primary profit center is its sleeping rooms division, with the catering department usually being the second most profitable department. Consequently, all hotel departments are generally organized and administered to maximize the sales and profits of sleeping rooms and catered functions. There are two general types of catering department organizations. In one form, the department is organized in such a way that all catering personnel are under the supervision of the property's food and beverage director.

The food and beverage director is responsible for the kitchens, restaurant outlets, and banquet operations, as well as for client solicitation and service. Within this structure, catering must secure the right to sell function space from the sales department, which controls meeting space. Sales managers are often reluctant to call their clients and ask them to release space they are holding as part of a meeting they have booked. Meetings are often booked years in advance, and savvy meeting planners, not knowing all of their space needs that far ahead, will institute a "hold all space" clause in their contracts.

In such an organizational structure, convention service managers are primarily responsible for room setup, but not for food or beverages. Alternatively, the catering department may be organized so that catering personnel are under the supervision of the sales and marketing director, with other employees, especially banquet servers, still reporting to the food and beverage director. In this situation there is generally a director of catering and convention services, who must work closely with the director of sales and marketing as well as with the food and beverage director.

Within this structure, catering managers and convention service are in the same department, both taking care of the food, beverage, and room setup needs of clients. The convention service managers do not sell the event, but take over client business booked by sales and marketing. They handle the planning and logistics of any meals or receptions and develop the appropriate service procedures needed to plan and implement successful and profitable catered events. In this scenario, most selling is "up$elling," or trying to get the client to purchase a more expensive meal, wine, or service.

Catering managers then sell shortterm food and beverage events to the local market or to functions without sleeping rooms, such as weddings, local banquets, and the like. With the revenue of catering being the responsibility of the marketing director, rather than the food and beverage director, sales managers are more likely to call clients to have rooms released for local banquets. In the second type of organizational pattern, the sales and marketing and food and beverage directors split the workload and coordinate catering sales and service.

In other facilities, the catering department handles all food and beverage service, and convention services personnel take care of all nonfood logistics, such as function room setups and teardowns, sleeping room arrangements, and so forth. There are advantages and disadvantages with each organizational form. The major advantages associated with the organizational forms are as follows:

— *Increased efficiency*: Clients work with one designated person who has authority to oversee the event from inception to completion. Last-minute requests and changes can be implemented quickly.

— *Isolated responsibility*: Responsibility is assigned to one person. Management and clients know exactly whom to contact if questions arise. This is a very critical position, in that the contact person is responsible for translating a client's needs and wishes into reality.

— *Job enrichment*: A person in charge of an event enjoys more variety than does a person involved with only one or two aspects.

— *Repeat patronage:* When clients deal with one person, there are additional opportunities to solicit repeat patronage and referrals.

— *Improved communications*: Because there are fewer persons on the communications chain, ambiguities and misinterpretations should be minimal.

The following are the major disadvantages of the organizational forms:

— *Excessive workload*: One person may not have enough hours in the day to perform all the necessary tasks.

— *Too many bosses*: The food and beverage department cannot be totally isolated; it must interact to some degree with the sales and marketing department. Unfortunately, this overlap may violate established chain-of-command policies unless the relationships are spelled out clearly.

— *Lack of specialization*: It is difficult to train one person to be expert in so many areas. However, if the catering manager is only the information point of exchange between clients and all other facility services, this potential problem can be minimized.

— *Excessive delegation*: If one person is not expert in all areas, the odds are that he or she will delegate responsibility freely. This can defeat the positive aspects of including all tasks under one person's direction. It also can confuse catering staff members.

As a general rule, catering department organization will be influenced by the support of upper management and

(1) the size of the facility,

(2) the types of functions catered,

(3) corporate policy, and

(4) the overall level of service offered by the facility.

Catering typically handles all food and beverage requirements, and convention service handles all nonfood arrangements.

Qualifications of Job Candidates

A job specification contains the qualities sought in a job candidate. Before hiring a catering department employee, a manager generally looks for at least five major qualities:

Technical Skills

Ideally, catering employees will have knowledge and skills in food and beverage preparation and service. At the very least, they must have an aptitude to learn and become familiar with the items on your menus and your services so that they can respond adequately to client inquiries.

It is required that most, if not all, catering employees have excellent sales skills. For some job positions, the primary qualification is the ability to sell. For instance, a sales representative's major asset is his or her ability to sell. However, even those employees primarily involved with guest service should have the ability to up$ell clients. They should be able to encourage clients to purchase additional, or higher quality, products and services, thereby increasing catering profits.

Communications skills are absolutely essential for catering staff members. Each function is a unique undertaking. There is no standard pattern or event template. Consequently, open and intelligible communications are critical to the success of a catered event. It is important for staff to be sufficiently articulate to communicate effectively with the host, the guests, and other staff members.

Conceptual Skills

As much as possible, catering department employees must be able to view the entire catering function and not see things exclusively from the perspective of their particular jobs. For instance, a banquet chef must appreciate the ceremonies involved with a wedding function and not ignore them when preparing and coordinating food courses.

Catering staff members must be able to take a client's "vision" of the function (including needs, wishes, purpose of the function, and budgetary constraints) and develop an event (through negotiations) consistent with this vision that can be delivered effectively and efficiently by the catering department. The planned catered event must meet the client's requirements.

Interpersonal Skills

Customer-contact skills are extremely important in the hospitality industry. Getting along with people, and satisfying them while simultaneously making a profit, is a challenge that must be met and overcome by all catering staff members. Unlike technical and conceptual skills, these skills generally cannot be taught-they are inherent. As Ellsworth Statler, founder of Statler Hotels, said once in the late 1800s, "Hire only good-natured people."

Other characteristics that managers look for in job candidates depend on the type of position and company policies. For instance, if the facility has a promotion-from-within policy, a manager will seek a job candidate who has the ability and desire to advance and grow with the company.

Policies of Catering Department

The facility must establish policies to guide the catering department's relations with clients. Typical policies include the following considerations.

— *Food and beverage prices*: It is a good idea to note that any listed prices are subject to change; in other words, the caterer should not assume responsibility if potential clients are viewing outdated menus. Caterers usually note that published menu prices are subject to change unless firm price guarantees are negotiated and included in a catering contract. If competitive bids are being prepared, all prices must be computed according to standard compan

— *Gratuities or service charges.* These are automatic charges added to the catering prices. Most properties add a 15 to 19 percent gratuity to the bill. You cannot assume that all clients are aware of these traditional charges: They must be informed about them up front.

— *Tips*. These are voluntary gifts. Some clients will want to tip some or all employees if they receive exceptional service. If you have a no-tipping policy, however, clients must know about it. Most government-owned facilities do not allow tipping.

— *Deposits*. The deposit procedures must be spelled out clearly. Clients must be informed of the amount that must be paid, when it must be tendered, and how it will be applied to the final billing.

— *Refunds*. Although no one likes to broach a negative subject, it is important to detail your refund policies and procedures in advance.

— *Guarantees*. A client must usually give a firm guarantee (guest count) two or three days in advance of the event. The facility will prepare food for that number of guests, plus a stipulated percentage over the guarantee to accommodate any guests who decide to attend at the last minute. For instance, most facilities will agree to handle the guaranteed number of guests and to overset about 3 to 5 percent, up to a maximum number-for example, 5 percent over or up to 100 persons maximum.

If the function is very large, a facility generally uses a sliding scale guarantee. For instance, although it may agree to a 5 percent overset for parties up to 500 persons, it may agree to accommodate only a 3 percent overage for parties in excess of 500.

Negotiating guarantees is a very tricky undertaking. The wise catering executive ensures that clients understand clearly the facility's position. Guarantees, as well as deposits, refund policies, miscellaneous charges, menu prices, and so forth, should always be spelled out very clearly in the catering contract. Some caterers require a client to initial each line item to indicate understanding.

Minimum purchase policy requires a client to purchase a minimum amount of catering services if he or she wants to book one or more events. For example, some big hotels in Las Vegas will not allow a convention to block out meeting room space unless there is a corresponding minimum amount of food and beverage business guaranteed. This food and beverage minimum is based on a set amount per guest room night.

Setup charges. If they are not included in the food and beverage menu prices, clients must be told in advance about these extra charges. A large function does not ordinarily incur additional setup charges; however, small groups may be subject to them. Extra charges can accrue if a room needs a fast turnover and extra labor must be called in to accomplish the job.

Most facilities will charge clients rent for the use of function rooms if they are used for meetings and other events that do not include significant food and beverage sales. For instance, there may be a charge for a room if the event does not generate at least $35 per person for food and/or beverage. The rental rate is usually calculated to cover the fixed overhead and provide a fair profit for the caterer. Some facilities have a sliding scale, with the charge depending on the dollar amount being generated.

Other extra charges. Depending on the size of the function, a facility may add on extra charges for bartenders, cashiers, valet parking, coat-checking facilities, and directional displays. If clients require additional labor because their functions are scheduled to last longer than normal, they will usually be assessed a service charge to cover the extra payroll cost (sometimes calculated as man-hour overtime).

Clients who have established credit ratings are usually allowed to put up a minimum deposit and pay the remaining balance within an allotted time, generally 30 days. Clients without credit approval usually must put up a large deposit and pay the remaining balance at least 2 days prior to the event or immediately after the function ends. Clients who are somewhere between having an established credit rating and no credit rating normally must provide a deposit and pay the remaining balance at the end of the catered event.

Outside food and beverage. Most, if not all, facilities will not allow clients to bring in their own food and beverage supplies. In most situations, the facility's liquor license, liability insurance, health permit, and/or business license forbids the use of personal products.

If the law and the facility allow clients to bring in their own products, there is usually a charge for setup service. For instance, if a client is allowed to bring in his or her own liquor, there may be a standard, one-time corkage fee for the service, or the facility may charge a standard fee for each drink prepared and served.

The facility must ensure that clients realize that the pertinent liquor laws will not be suspended during their catered events. For instance, wedding hosts may not see anything wrong with serving wine to an underage guest at a private party. However, the law does not make this distinction. The same is true for service to visibly intoxicated guests; they cannot legally be served by the banquet staff. If clients request self-service bars, some caterers will require them to sign a waiver of liquor liability so that they are not held responsible for the actions of the guests.

This type of waiver is necessary because, in the case of self-service, the facility does not have bartenders and cocktail servers onsite to monitor underage drinking and service to visibly intoxicated guests. Because of this potential liability, many caterers do not permit self-service bars.

Many clients need to use their own signs, displays, decorations, and/or demonstrations at booked events. The facility usually reserves the right to approve these items and to control their placement and location. If clients are allowed to have displays, the facility usually expects the clients to be responsible for any damage done and any extraordinary cleanup that may result.

The removal of confetti, rice, and birdseed can pose a challenge. Similar restrictions may apply to other materials, such as paper products, decorations, and equipment. Tape and tacks can damage walls, and some items can be fire hazards.

Responsibility for loss and/or damage. Personal property brought into the facility by guests are not usually covered by the facility's insurance policies. Consequently, clients and their guests must be informed of this policy, and agree to it, before receiving permission to use their own property.

A facility usually expects clients to agree to in-demnify it against any claims, losses, and/or damages, except those due solely to the negligence and/or willful misconduct of the facility staff. The facility also wants protection from claims made by outside service contractors, such as florists, decorators, or audiovisual (AV) firms engaged by clients. Furthermore, clients are expected to stipulate that by paying the final bill, they agree that there are no disputes with the products and services received.

There are times when a facility will be unable to perform through no fault of its own. For instance, bad weather, a strike, a labor dispute, or another circumstance may hamper the facility's ability to service its clients. Consequently, clients must agree to hold harmless the facility under uncontrollable conditions of this type.

A policy regarding substitutions is similar to the policy on uncontrollable acts. Occasionally, supply problems may force a caterer to substitute menu products, or it may be necessary to move a function from one meeting room to another. For instance, an out-door event may have to be moved indoors at the last minute because of inclement weather. Or a contractor's strike may force the facility to substitute other space of comparable size and quality. Although few of us want to think about these potential problems, clients must be advised in advance that they could occur. Always provide proper advance communication with clients so surprises do not anger them.

A facility may require a client to provide additional security for his or her event. For instance, a meeting of diamond dealers would be expected to schedule a great deal of personal security that is provided by or approved by the facility. Alternatively, the facility may reserve the right to hire additional security guards and bill the event host. If you outsource valet parking, always check references to ensure the security of your patron's automobiles.

Some functions may need to be approved and/or licensed by the local government licensing agency. For instance, a function that has a cover charge may need a temporary admission license. The facility should reserve the right to refuse service to any client who does not hold the appropriate licenses and permits prior to the event.

Challenges of Catering Services

Some of the major challenges encountered by the catering department.

Marketing the catering department's services. A great deal of time must be spent in this effort to distinguish your facility in the minds of potential clients. Clients tend to perceive caterers as interchangeable as buses: There is always another one available who can handle their needs. You will need to battle this perception constantly.

Excessive amount of time spent with clients. Unfortunately, only a small number of persons and groups contacted will end up purchasing catered events. Moreover, once business is booked, a great deal of time must be spent planning and coordinating the events. Although some clients need more handholding than others, the wise catering executive will expect to devote much time to these tasks.

To maximize available catering sales time, savvy caterers learn to determine how much time is necessary and/or appropriate to spend with a prospective client, who may be a serious buyer or merely a casual shopper for catering services.

Unique demands. All functions have unique demands. For instance, refreshment breaks are sometimes permanently set, but clients may not have a particular schedule in mind and merely wish to visit the refreshment area when time permits. This is especially true in conference centers, where attendees can break at will. Consequently, set-ups must to be freshened periodically, which requires an employee to be constantly alert to fluctuating needs.

Difficulty in costing out and pricing certain functions. Special requests and last-minute needs will cost more because of the special circumstances. The aforementioned refreshment breaks fall into this category. Because the demands these events present cannot always be predicted in advance, function hosts usually must wait until a final accounting is made by the catering department. This can cause ill will among clients, especially those who are on a tight budget and would appreciate price guarantees.

Ethical traps. Sometimes a catering department may encounter conflict-of-interest dilemmas. For example, clients who need outside contractors, such as tour buses, entertainers, and decorators, may ask the caterer for a recommendation. The facility, always mindful of its image and reputation, will tend to recommend only a few outside contractors that can fill the bill adequately. However, such favoritism may be perceived by some as shady dealing.

Responsibility greater than authority. It is very important to determine in advance who is responsible for each part of an event. For instance, a convention may want to hire its own band but simultane-ously expect the facility to coordinate the details. This can easily lead to misunderstandings and client dissatisfaction unless everything is spelled out clearly.

Time pressures. The catering department is a pressure cooker. It seems as if everything must be ready "yesterday." Catering personnel must learn to work well within time constraints.

Working with and coordinating with other departments and outside agencies. Proper advance planning is necessary to avoid service glitches that could cause guest dissatisfaction. Caterers must cultivate the ability to communicate effectively.

Maintaining qualified staff members. Many catering departments experience severe volume swings. For instance, convention centers pose a unique challenge in terms of volume and staffing. One day you may have a breakfast for 5,000, which requires a lot of labor. But you may not have another similar function for two weeks; as a result, it is very difficult to keep qualified employees, many of whom prefer more predictable work schedules.

The lack of technical foodservice skills. Many caterers today, both men and women, have less knowledge about food than ever before. They are increasingly reliant on chefs and food and beverage directors for advice. This would not be a major problem if standardized menus were used consistently; however, things are more trendy these days, there is more competition, and many clients want custom menus and something special. This can make it difficult to respond quickly to unusual customer requests.

A potential client may become restless with the catering executive who needs to confer constantly with other food and beverage people in the organization. However, an executive's confidence and poise can transcend the bonds of ignorance. Instead of dismay, a potential client may be quite pleased with the executive who may not have the answer at the very moment, but who promises to get it quickly.

Helth and Safety Threats

Statistics have proved that bad management practices cause accidents and cost money, time and effort. Accident rates in the catering industry have been getting steadily worse over the last six years. The rate of major injury is now 54% higher than in 1986. Over 69% of major injuries result from slipping and tripping or falling on the same level or from contact with harmful or hot substances. The rate of accidents which are not major, but lead to three or more days off work has more than doubled over the last six years. These figures represent costs both in terms of pain and suffering for individuals and in direct costs to employers.

Recent studies across a range of industries suggest that for each accident resulting in an injury leading to three days off work there are seven less serious injuries and 189 accidents resulting in damage to property. Accidents can result in costs representing up to 8.5% of a company's turnover, and yet 70% of these accidents could have been prevented by improved health and safety management.

Individual workplaces will, of course, exhibit their own patterns of risk, but the main causes of accidents and ill health in the catering industry are:

— slips, trips and falls;

— lifting and manual handling;

— contact with hot surfaces and harmful substances;

— dermatitis;

— work-related upper limb disorders.

Most accidents can be prevented by good management and supervision combined with effective training, which makes accident prevention no different from any other aspect of running a successful business. Careful thought and planning applied to those areas of catering where the risks are highest should help to prevent accidents and reduce costs. It will also show enforcement officers that you are going down the right route towards complying with health and safety legislation.

Owners and managers have clearly defined legal duties about training employees. The law requires every employer and self-employed person to consider the health and safety training needs of themselves and all employees, including new recruits, part-timers and temporary or agency staff. It is important to appreciate that time and effort spent in ensuring staff are working safely and understand the reasons for good practices is likely to:

— save the business time and money: there will be less money and time wasted in staff accidents, damaged equipment, damage to premises and wasted resources;
— improve staff morale and feelings of security, leading to improved service, commitment and motivation.

Good management of health and safety can only be achieved with the co-operation of the workforce. It is vital that your employees know what is expected of them and are aware of any risks to their health and safety that may arise at work and any safe systems of work that are applied. The co-operation of the workforce is likely to be more constructive if you consult with them about developing health and safety measures. Where you recognise a trade union, safety representatives must be consulted about the health and safety arrangements before action is taken. Where trade unions are not involved the workforce should be encouraged to appoint its own safety representatives.

Involving safety representatives helps ensure that health and safety measures will be effective in practice. Health and safety will not be a burden if managed properly. Managing health and safety effectively:

— ensures it is not a burden;
— keeps costs to a minimum and can bring savings;
— prevents injury and ill health to your business' most important resource: people;

— reduces the likelihood of civil claims.

Effective management of health and safety can best be achieved by:

— realising it is an integral and essential part of business management;

— identifying the main risk areas and taking action on those first;

— setting yourself clear targets, for example to train staff and to clearly allocate responsibilities;

— supervising adequately;

— sconsulting staff at all stages.

In most catering situations, local authority enforcement officers are responsible for the enforcement of health and safety legislation. Inspectors from HSE look after health and safety in catering facilities in institutions such as hospitals, schools etc. The role of the enforcement officer is not just to enforce the law but also to promote health and safety, give advice on the law and how to comply with it and advise on other sources of information - for example, a series of booklets available from HSE. Additionally, many local authorities either arrange or facilitate health and safety training. So, enforcement officers are there to help businesses and promote health and safety.

You may have read that a number of new Regulations are in force, dealing with a range of health and safety issues, from manual handling through to safety management. The aim of the Committee is to highlight requirements which are particularly important to catering establishments, and this will be done in further information sheets in this series. However, set out below is an outline of what the law requires in general. The law requires you to ensure, as far as is reasonably practicable, the health and safety of yourself and others who may be affected by what you do or fail to do. The duties extend to people who:

— work for you, including agency, casual, part-time and trainee workers and subcontractors;

— use workplaces you provide;

— are allowed to use your equipment;

— visit your premises;

— may be affected by your work;

— use your professional services.

You may provide catering services to other employers at their workplace. The law requires all employers sharing the same workplace to co-operate and co-ordinate on health and safety. The law applies to all work premises and everyone at work - employee, supervisor, manager, director or self-employed - has duties. In practical terms you must identify the risks in your workplace and, as far as is reasonably practicable, take steps to reduce or eliminate them. In some cases legislation related to the Health and Safety at Work Act may require specific measures to be taken.

Gas safety Issues

Gas appliances, flues, pipe work and safety devices must be maintained in a safe condition. They should be inspected by a competent person in accordance with current industry practice. Periods between inspections may vary depending on the equipment and its use and should follow manufacturer's recommendations, but as a general rule annual inspections will be a reasonable minimum frequency.

In addition to duties to maintain appliances, flues and pipe work, landlords must have all appliances and flues checked every 12 months by a CORGI-registered business and provide tenants with a copy of the report within 28 days. This applies to residential accommodation including hotels, guest houses, bed sits, communal kitchens, tied accommodation, holiday boats and caravans and staff accommodation even on industrial or other premises not otherwise subject to the Regulations. So this duty may apply in certain areas of the hospitality industry.

All catering and hospitality staff who use gas equipment should be trained in its proper use and common-sense daily visual inspection for obvious faults. This will include such things as damaged pipe work and connections, inoperative flame supervision devices, missing restraints on equipment needing them for stability, inoperative locks on castors of mobile equipment and smells of escaping gas. Routine tasks such as connecting and disconnecting plug-in gas connections to appliances when moving for cleaning or changing LPG cylinders or hoses can be carried out by people who are not CORGI-registered, but they must be competent. It should be noted that the installation of an appliance with a plug-in gas connection should only be carried out by a CORGI-registered person, including the safety examinations prescribed in GSIUR.

The majority of catering kitchens use mechanical ventilation systems to create a comfortable working environment that promotes health and safety at work and encourages good practice for hygiene and food safety. These systems are designed to remove the products from the cooking processes and discharge them to a safe external location, normally via a canopy installed over the cooking appliances. Make-up air is supplied in the form of natural ventilation through air vents, louvres or serving hatches etc. In some instances, ventilation systems also provide mechanical make-up air to the kitchen as well as extraction. It is important to recognise that ventilation systems serve several purposes apart from removal of combustion products. They:

— introduce sufficient clean, cool air and remove excess hot air from the cooking area, to enable the occupants to breathe adequately and provide comfortable conditions;

— prevent incomplete combustion of gas and the consequent production of harmful carbon monoxide;

— dilute and remove odours, vapours and steam from the cooking process.

When installing second-hand ovens and similar enclosed burner equipment such as steamers, these should be provided with flame supervision devices and appropriately upgraded gas controls. In practice, as employers have had nine years to comply, ovens should only be operating without flame supervision devices in exceptional cases. Generally speaking, all ovens should have been upgraded or replaced by now.

The Standard also states that all burners on second-hand equipment being installed should be fitted with flame supervision devices where this is reasonably practicable. This will apply to all other open burners on second-hand equipment. Each fixed appliance should have a single manual means of isolation for servicing or cleaning purposes and pipes shall be located to leave a space of at least 25 mm between the pipe and the wall in order to assist cleaning.

Any user of gas who has any concerns about the safety of their installation should not wait until the next routine maintenance visit or breakdown, but seek urgent advice from a competent gas operative. This process should take into account the procedures, training, systems of work and warning notices etc that are being applied, in addition to the condition and use of the existing ventilation system.

These range from immediate condemnation of the appliance to simple notification that it does not comply with current standards. If a gas operative does this, they should give the person responsible for the kitchen information about the new standard and the practicability of upgrading the installation.

Factors that will increase the risk include:

— evidence that ventilation system is not used or is unreliable;

— small room volume;

— obvious poor design/maintenance of ventilation system (long, convoluted ducts, broken fans, leaking ductwork, visible escape of cooking fumes/steam etc);

— lack of user awareness of the effect of using gas appliances without adequate ventilation;

— poor general ventilation to dilute any spillage of products;

— extensive use of gas-fired appliances for long periods;

— ageing system/installation;

— operation of Type B appliances.

Factors that will reduce risk include:

— good natural ventilation;

— satisfactory fume removal through ventilation ductwork by natural draught alone;
— well maintained ventilation system;
— good user awareness of risks and proper, documented procedures for using additional ventilation;
— minimal use of gas-fired appliances;
— modern ventilation system;
— large room size;
— clear, permanent notices warning that appliances must not be used without the ventilation system in operation.

Direct airflow measurements have traditionally been regarded as the most reliable means of monitoring that ventilation ducting is working properly, but in catering ducting, fat and grease build-up can cause these to fail so that pressure switches with no exposed moving parts are now accepted as the best solution. Provided these are suitably located and ducting is kept adequately clean, switch failure and ventilation shut down should be avoided.

Properly functioning ventilation systems are becoming a more important feature in ensuring kitchen safety. So the use of a properly designed and fully specified system, with a record of its design performance characteristics, will make it considerably easier for both owners of kitchens and gas operatives to assess whether fumes are being adequately removed and fresh air and combustion air are being provided.

Many more appliances are now fitted with castors to allow movement for cleaning as a result of the increasing demands of food hygiene laws. Careful installation allowing cleaning without moving the appliance may permit fixing of such appliances where there are risks of splashing from hot liquids (particularly oil) during movement and flexible gas connectors may not be necessary. If appliances containing hot liquids have to be moved, they must be fitted with lockable castors that are regularly maintained.

Vehicles using gas-fired cooking appliances, such as fish and chip vans or travelling barbecues, usually use LPG. Appliances and any pilot lights should not be lit while the vehicle is in motion. This increases the chance of the flame going out and some vehicles have exploded due to this. There are some exceptions to this such as specialised vehicles for 'meals on wheels' which have special safeguards installed. .

Some kitchens have these installed. Domestic models are not designed or tested for use in the generally much harsher commercial working environment and should not be used. If installed, carbon monoxide detectors shall give an audible alarm and be linked with an automatic gas shut-off system. This should be fail-safe and require manual intervention to restore the gas supply. They should only be regarded as a secondary back up. The primary safeguard remains provision of adequate ventilation to ensure complete combustion of gas and removal of combustion products.

A number of restaurants use a length of flattened copper pipe connected to a flexible hose and mains gas rather than a hand-held torch for such work and other activities. Only blowtorches of an approved proprietary design, which have been installed and tested by a CORGI-registered installer, should be used. When not in use, the blowtorch should be disconnected from the gas supply and the gas sealed off. A self-sealing, quick-release fitting installed downstream of an installation valve may be suitable for this application.

Sources of fires in ductwork above open flame gas appliances include flambéing, flame-grilling and stir-frying. Ductwork should be regularly cleaned to prevent build-up of grease and fat. This can be an unpleasant and awkward task and great care is needed to ensure a proper job is done as experience has shown this is often skimped.

2

Managing Food and Beverage Operations

Hotel guests generally enjoy the convenience of food and beverage outlets, hut when given the chance, they frequently choose a known brand off the premises, leaving a hotel for nearby restaurant chains. In the process, they take much-desired dining dollars with them. As customers become more brand —aware, competition for food and beverage business continues to grow in importance for many hotels.

From the hotel's perspective, a joint venture or outsourcing arrangement can provide a combination of restaurant skills and brand strength, often supported by national advertising. Hotels adding branded restaurants have reported improved food and beverage volume, including room service sales, as well as an attendant increase in occupancy and average rate. In a period of hospitality industry consolidation, branded restaurants may become a point of differentiation among hotel properties.

Restaurant companies, of course, also stand to gain from this flurry of alliances. In today's market, many companies are being forced to look outside traditional development options and to consider new types of locations. Given these benefits, it is surprising there is not more outsourcing of food and beverage in the hotel industry.

During the early 1990s, businesses faced the difficult task of assessing procedural strengths and weaknesses to trim fat and streamline processes. Outsourcing non-critical activities allowed companies to extend their organisational core competencies. The hospitality and leisure industry was no exception to this trend. During the past few years, hotels have been called on to assess their core competencies, while attempting to shed responsibility for non-core activities.

Core competencies can be defined as those unique disciplines that confer competitive advantage, motivating customers to buy a company's goods and services over those of a competitor. As this decade comes to a close, businesses are further dividing the non-core segment into two categories: "essential non-core" and "non-essential non-core." Those activities that are both non-core and non-essential are being shut down. Processes that are essential, but "non-core," become prime candidates for outsourcing. Providing quality rooms and guest services remains a hotel's primary function.

The food and beverage function, however, commands attention because of its importance to guest satisfaction and brand management. Many hoteliers, however, make the mistake of thinking that it takes the same competencies to operate a restaurant as it does to run a hotel. In actual fact, the restaurant business requires a different set of skills, including more attention to detail, than rooms management.

By reengineering food and beverage operations, hotel management has the opportunity to redirect energies from the restaurant business and focus efforts on enhancing hotel operations and profitability and, potentially, shareholder value. This raises important questions for management. When does it make financial and operational sense to outsource food and beverage? If the decision is made to outsource, how can a partnership be structured most successfully?

Outsourcing Partnerships

Outsourcing partnerships typically bring together organisations with diverse capabilities. Understanding what each side of the equation requires to succeed is essential. This important guideline applies whether a hotel owner is considering outsourcing all or part of its food and beverage operations to a restaurant chain, or merely outsourcing its coffee shop to a local restaurateur.

Historically, restaurant chains have been strict about the demographics and economic indicators in a market before committing to a location. And until recently, there was no shortage of suitable sites. Prime demographic indicators include a mix of office space, upper-middle class residences, and upscale apartments with higher-income professionals looking for an element of fun. If a potential restaurant site was not viewed as a "home run" location, a restaurateur would typically pass on a development opportunity. Due to increased competition and a limited number of prime sites, restaurant companies have found they must go further afield than in the past, breaking traditional biases about what locations work.

Until recently, hotels have been reluctant to outsource their food and beverage operations - or single restaurants. Traditionally, hotel management viewed food and beverage operations as a low margin or unprofitable service required to enhance guest satisfaction. As such, food and beverage profitability was always examined with a mentality of "minimizing a loss."

As a way to rationalise an unprofitable track record, hotel management often convinced itself that there was insufficient demand for profitable food and beverage operations. In addition, as hotels emerged from the last recession and downturn in hotel profitability, emphasis was placed on the renovation of guestrooms, lobbies and banquet space over food and beverage outlets. Based on historical trends, renovation priority has consistently been given to profit-generating guestrooms over unprofitable food and beverage operations.

Additionally, hotels opting to create a new concept or introduce an existing, branded concept may find start-up costs to he exorbitant. Estimated costs of upgrading a food and beverage outlet to a chain's specified standards range from $500,000 to $1.5 million, depending on the extent of renovation and equipment purchases required. Of course, outsourcing operations to a local restaurateur would likely cost far less. The hotel, however, would not benefit from the brand recognition associated with a larger, more established name in the marketplace. Lastly, hotel management companies earning fees based on gross revenue may be reluctant to reduce the base on which their management fee is calculated. This may prompt hotel owners and managers to reassess their management position. Frequently the parties agree to either renegotiate revenue-based fee percentages or include revenues earned by third-party food and beverage operators in the management fee calculations.

Despite the issues associated with outsourcing of food and beverage operations, there are compelling reasons for hotels to consider this option. Brand strength and competitive positioning for the hotel property are among the most important.

Branding and Repositioning

Why is it that guests often prefer to patronise known brands rather than a hotel's stand-alone food and beverage outlet? While consumers are more brand aware than ever before, research suggests there may even be a perceived stigma associated with dining in a hotel restaurant. Integrating a branded concept into a hotel is a way to minimize the stigma, bringing guests back to the hotel outlets and reducing internal costs. Additionally, familiar dining concepts seem to put travelers at ease. Customers who are away from home and out of their element are comforted by the availability and consistency that accompanies a known brand name product.

In 1995 Choice Hotels surveyed its full service hotels and learned that most of its properties experienced a great deal of difficulty keeping restaurants profitable. Reported food expenditures of 40 to 50 percent of their food and beverage revenues, accompanied by labour costs of 45 to 50 percent, made it virtually impossible to generate a profit, according to Barbara Shuster, Director of Choice Hotels International's Choice Picks programme. To combat this trend, select Choice hotels implemented a food court concept in the food and beverage area, and were surprised to see food and labour costs on food and beverage revenues drop to an average of 32 percent and 28 percent, respectively.

In addition to brand identity, most operators find that guests are not only more willing to patronise high-street brands conveniently situated within the hotel, but they are also willing to pay more for the privilege of dining with a familiar concept. Increased willingness to dine coupled with increased willingness to spend results in increased revenues.

Hotels introducing a branded restaurant into their property often experience higher external traffic. Market exposure translates into increased outlet revenue and enhanced customer perception of the food and beverage outlet brand name, as well as enhanced customer perception of the hotel itself. Thus the net result of rebranding and repositioning can be increased profit and enhanced shareholder value.

Making it Work

Before taking the plunge into the world of outsourced or reengineered food and beverage operations, hotel management must take several factors into consideration:

— *Competition*: No outsourcing arrangement will work, unless there is market demand. Competitive analysis should include restaurants in neighboring hotels, as well as stand-alone restaurants in the area. Profitability issues and pricing a new outlet also must be considered in the market context. Many hotels find that the brand name restaurant buys recognition in the customer 5 mind and creates a draw for business. The partnered restaurant sets the hotel apart from other hotels in the area and segment by providing a strong competitive and marketing advantage.

— *Marketing*: The hotelier and restaurateur must establish responsibility for marketing of the new concept. Frequently hotels agree to advertise the operator in the guestrooms, although the outlet typically absorbs the cost of signage in the rooms and throughout the hotel. Additionally, the restaurateur typically assumes responsibility and accountability for all external advertising.

— *Guest expectations*: The goal of outsourcing food and beverage operations is to enhance profitability by increasing internal as well as external traffic, without losing the current customer base. It is essential to consider guest reaction to the change in food and beverage concept. If a negative reaction is anticipated, a hotelier risks losing its customer base and thus future earning potential to the competition.

— *Management styles*: It is important to look at both the local and corporate management styles of both the hotelier and restaurateur, Incompatibility of the two styles could result in a rocky relationship and tumultuous times. In order to avoid this friction, some hotels have found it advantageous to appoint the general manager of the restaurant to the hotel's executive team, thereby creating a sense of responsibility and belonging and enhancing relationships throughout the organisation.

— *Terms of the Contract*: The operational terms of the contract must be set out in detail. Quality standards and monitoring mechanisms should be detailed to ensure that the restaurant is operated at a standard that is acceptable and complementary to that of the hotel. Additionally, hours of restaurant operation, including room service, are critical specifications. As breakfast is typically a money - generating activity, and frequently not one that restaurant chain operators are accustomed to serving, many hoteliers prefer to maintain responsibility for this meal. However, concessions affecting profitability occasionally need to be made in order to solidify a working relationship.

A successful outsourcing relationship involves first and foremost trust and cohesion between the two partners. Of course, operational terms must be clearly detailed and make economic sense for both parties. While the requirements of a restaurant chain may be more stringent and costly than those of an independent restaurant operator, the basic tenets of a trusting partnership, complementary levels of quality, compatible clientele and a location with sufficient demand to justify a restaurant operation are all necessary. Successful implementation of an food and beverage outsourcing partnership can result in enhanced brand recognition and profitability for both the hotelier and the restaurateur.

Structuring an Outsourcing Partnership

— *Leasing* : A hotel leases a room or section of the hotel, preferably with self-contained back-of-the-house areas in exchange for a flat fee and/or a percentage of sales. Statistics are not available for this type of transaction, as leasing deals vary depending on the area of space being leased, the brand being introduced into the market, the location of the hotel and agreements that may have been established by a head office. The hotel benefits by receiving a guaranteed rent, plus a revenue "top-up" each month. The landlord, however, loses control of food and beverage operations. Management must agree to let someone else run the show.

— *Franchising:* This option suits a hotel seeking to change a restaurant concept without investing in an internal and potentially untested concept. The hotel buys an established brand and system for a fee. The process begins with an upfront payment - a buy-in to the right to operate a better known and more profitable concept. Frequently, the franchisor requires the hotel to make an additional payment for a capital investment, requiring a purchase of specified equipment. Under the franchising terms, the hotel pays the franchisor a royalty fee, usually based on a percentage of sales, for the privilege of using the name and resources. Throughout the relationship, it is the franchisees responsibility to ensure that hotel staff is adequately trained to assure quality consistent with other branded sites. Marriott International was one of the first major hotel chains to enter into food and beverage franchising arrangements, with a 1989 franchising partnership with Pizza Hut. Marriott has since introduced Pizza Hut outlets and in-room dining options at many of its properties throughout the world.

— *Joint Venture*: This is a variant of franchising and contracting. The hotelier creates a strategic alliance with a known, successful restaurateur. The two parties create a separate financial company, which is appointed as the lessee of the restaurant. The new organisation, the restaurant lessee., then outsources the food and beverage operations to the restaurateur. Typically the hotel provides the capital expenditures and the restaurateur brings intellectual property and expertise. The two parties share the successes and the related profits. For example, Marco Pierre White formed a joint venture with Granada hotels valued at £2 million to provide food and beverage services at seven select Forte hotels in the UK. The new organisation, MPW Criterion, will reengineer the way select Granada hotel food and beverage outlets do business. Additionally, before its merger with Starwood Lodging, ITT Corporation, owner of Sheraton Hotels and Caesar's Casinos, formed a partnership with Planet Hollywood International to develop, construct and manage Planet Hollywood - themed casinos in Las Vegas and Atlantic City. The two parties were also entertaining the idea of converting existing hotel outlets into Planet Hollywood restaurants.

— *Proprietary Brands*: Hotel chains can create a proprietary brand, introducing the concept into all of its properties. This approach appeals to guests who enjoy consistency throughout a hotel chain. However, it is difficult to gain wider customer identity outside of the hotel properties. Marriott, for example, already has its own concepts in place, including JW's Steakhouse, Allie's American Grille and Champion's Bar. Likewise, Regal Hotels is growing its own brands, including Hard Edged and Morrisey's Pub, in several of its hotels as well as developing food and beverage solutions through its alliance with The Restaurant Partnership.

Recovering Food and Beverage

The recovery of the hotel industry since the doldrums of the early 1990s has been well documented. At first, limited new construction lead to steady growth in occupancy from year to year. Then, starting in 1994, the favorable balance of supply and demand allowed hotel managers to raise their room rates two to three times the pace of inflation. The net result has been a doubling of property level profits from 1991 to 1997.

Certainly, the strong growth in room rates has been the major impetus behind the rise in profits. However, not as frequently discussed has been the tremendous growth in profits generated by food and beverage departments.

With total food and beverage revenue growing 17.7 percent, and expenses growing at only 9.6 percent, f&b department profits have grown 54.5 percent from 1994 to 1997. Long thought of as a break-even operation at best, hotel food and beverage departments are now providing a significant contribution to the bottom line of a hotel.

Analyzing the detail, it is obvious that the majority of the improvement in department profitability has come from the sale and preparation of food, as opposed to alcoholic beverages.

Food revenues (not including other income), measured on a per-occupied-room basis, have grown 18.5 percent from 1994 to 1997. This growth rate does fall short of the 25.1 percent growth rate in ADR during the same period. However, it is still a remarkable statistic, considering the number of full-service hotels that have cut their number of outlets, limited their hours of service, or adopted other forms of food service (food courts, leased restaurants, etc.).

Concurrent with the rise in food sales has been a decline in the food cost percentage. From 1994 to 1997, the cost of food sold has declined from 30.9 percent of sales to 29.4 percent. This decline can be attributed to a shift towards serving items with a lower cost, as well as greater controls. Menus historically dominated by high-cost steaks and chops have been replaced with lower-cost, healthy items (salads, poultry, fish) and popular/ familiar foods (wraps, hamburgers, home-cooking).

Following the change in social habits, the growth in alcoholic beverage sales has been much more limited than the growth in food sales. Since 1994, beverage sales at hotels have grown a mere 5.2 percent when measured on a per-occupied-room basis. Unfortunately, the dollars a hotel spends to purchase the alcohol sold has increased 8.1 percent during the same period. Once an easy profit center for most hotels, hotel lounges are becoming less of a source for automatic money.

As creative as hotel food and beverage directors have become adjusting their menus, hours of operation, ambiance, and marketing techniques, the one component of food and beverage service that still remains rather large is labor. Total labor costs in the food and beverage department have remained relatively constant at approximately 42 percent from 1994 to 1997.

Like overall labor costs for hotels, total payroll and benefits in the food and beverage department have averaged a 4.2 percent annual growth rate since 1994. This rate of growth is approximately twice that of the national average annual growth rate for labor costs in all industries. Until hotels and restaurants are able to produce and serve meals with a "Jetsons-like" machine, the personal touch will always be a major component of food and beverage production and service.

Labor expenses and cost-of-goods-sold have historically been identified as the "prime costs" of operating a food and beverage department. Together, these two expenses have grown 15.5 percent between 1994 and 1997. During this same period, however, all the other costs associated with the operation of the food and beverage department have actually declined from $1,344 per-available room in 1994 to $1,070 in 1997. These other expenses include such items as laundry, china, glassware, silver, linen, and entertainment. It is apparent that restaurant, lounge, and banquet managers have focused on cutting expense items that are mostly fixed in nature.

The rental of guest rooms will continue to be the major source of income and profits for hotels that offer food and beverage service. Therefore, it is practical that the greater portion of management's time and resources should be allocated to the rooms department.

Since the recession of the 1990s, hotel owners have become much more sensitive to the fiscal health of their properties and no longer tolerate losses from any of the operating departments. Therefore, food and beverage managers will need to continue their effective turnaround of this area of the hotel that has historically been ignored and overlooked.

Selected Food and Beverage Growth Rates 1994 to 1997

Total food and beverage Revenue	17.7%
Salaries and Benefits	16.7%
Total Department Expenses	9.6%
Department Profits	54.5%

Food and Beverage Department Profits, Percent of Department Revenues	
1997	23.7%
1996	21.6%
1995	19.2%
1994	18.0%

Food and Beverage Cost of Goods Sold
Percentage of Revenue

Year	*Food*	*Beverage*
1997	29.4%	23.6%
1996	30.0%	23.6%
1995	30.7%	23.3%
1994	30.9%	22.9%

Food and Beverage Operation and Environment

It is not uncommon to hear, particularly among hotel owners and operators relatively new to the industry, that Food and Beverage (F&B) cannot make nay money and should be leased out if such facilities exist in a particular hotel. This, of course, begs a number of questions: How could a tenant make money of a landlord cannot, especially after paying rent? Why would a hotel owner with a major investment want an important interrelated business with a different business goals and possibly incompatible clientele in the building with minimal control over that other business.

While everyone will claim that food and beverage facilities are included in hotels to be profitable, we believe that should be secondary. The primary reason for an food and beverage facility is to enhance the potential revenues of the Rooms Department if the Hotel. This is particularly obvious with convention and resort hotels.

A good food and beverage operation, whether operated or leased, will allow more flexibility in marketing. This flexibility will help sell rooms during slow periods during the week or year. The presence of an food and beverage operation will allow the hotel to appeal to more market segments, thus giving the hotel a broader and more secure income base. An food and beverage operation should first be designed and concepted to maximize room revenue, secondly to do that profitably and third to appeal to non-hotel patrons,. The owner then needs to follow up with the same food and beverage marketing and management effort an lessee would invest, thus insuring success.

Recently we undertook an assignment to conduct an operational overview of what is physically a mid-priced full service hotel. It is generally operated a limited service, mid-priced hotel with a leased food and beverage operation. The hotel is affiliated with a well-known national brand, is in a major metropolitan area and is generally very competently managed. What follows are excerpts from our report regarding the leased food and beverage operation, its problems, their impact on the hotel, and some changes which should be implemented to minimize the detriment to the hotel:

Our expenses in the restaurants, recently leased to new operator, have been mediocre at best. There was one gentlemen walking around in his jacket on several occasions, believed to be either the manager or the lessee. None of the employees wear uniforms and this creates the impression of less-than-professional operation. On one occasion we to charge the bill to our room.

There was no attempt to verify that we registered or that we had credit available and could charge the restaurant. For instance, if we were cash paying guests, with only a minimal deposit for telephone charges, we should not be allowed to charge in the restaurant because the hotel has no ability to capture this charge. The restaurant should be given a list of guests with credit established to charge in the restaurant along with their room numbers.

Some recommendations for the case are given below:

The guest and restaurant patrons have the understandable impression that the restaurant is part of the hotel. They should to need to know otherwise. Therefore, the hotel's same standards of behavior, operation, and appearance need to be required of the lessee. It is crucial that the restaurant operation not detract from the rest of the hotel. At present, this is unfortunately the case. Uniforms with footwear and accessory standards, name tags, well groomed appearance, professionally done with tasteful supplementary signage and appropriate graphics must all be present. Employees must be held to behavior standards which contribute to the hotels image, not detract from it. The tenants lease includes the right to use the landlord's liquor license. In this case, it would be the liquor license owner and fee simple owner who would be sued in dram shop case. With this is mind, we strongly recommend that the restaurant owner be required to conduct server training for all current and d future employees on a regular basis and provide the landlord with documentation of that training. The documentation should include the course name, content, instructor and the signature of every employee in attendance. The lease for the restaurant space is predicated on the tenant's revenues. In order to maximize those revenues and therefore the income of the hotel, there should be some joint marketing efforts. These might include:

— Distributing restaurant discount coupons by the front desk staff at check-in with management's compliments

— Tenant cards in the guest rooms promoting the restaurant and its hours, providing room service along with fast items such as pizza.

— Packaging the hotel with meals for promotions during slow times.

— Penetrating commercial business by including a hot cooked to order breakfast in the room rate.

— Having professionally done menus for food and beverage service to the meeting rooms.

— Include a restaurant representative to executive committee meetings.

An Analysis of food and beverage and Hotels

In summary, we reported, the restaurant is not just an appendage to lease out and collect minimal rent from; it must be developed as an asset that contributes to the overall profitability of the enterprise. Leasing is a common answer among limited service operators, however the full benefit of the presence of the facility will never be realized under any scenario, if the two separate businesses are not marketed together at a positive standard.

This excerpt highlights some common operational problems experienced by hotels with leased food and beverage operations.

The marketing harmony between the two independent businesses will never be there to the same level there would be when these things are not major issues.

On the expense side the efficiencies of scale are missing. Before the tenant pays rent s/he must pay all the same expenses the owner would have to pay, regardless of how they might be allocated on the hotel's financial statement, plus separate accounting, insurance, etc. Many items would cost a lot more because of the lesser purchasing power. Credit card commissions are an example. Labor efficiencies are also lost. Why should the hotel's staff clean up a room service spill in the hall or remove trays from a room? If the food and beverage lease includes the equipment and furniture and possibly its maintenance what incentive does the lessee have to be careful and who buys replacement items and who owns them?

At the bottom line of any profit the tenant makes after lease payments is profit the hotel owner has forgone!

The most common conflict between the two businesses lies in the area of banquet booking. The leased food and beverage operator only cares about food and beverage revenues. S/he will book anything any amount of time in the future to maximize those revenues. The hotel's management normally would hold back on booking banquets without major rooms business associated with it in more to have that space available as an enticement to various forms of guest rooms business with meeting and banquet room needs. Clearly, there must be cutoffs, depending on business patterns, when the space is released for banquet business but never to the detriment of a lucrative group business. How does the hotel insure that food and beverage services group room business in a manner that enhances repeat business?

If the food and beverage tenant's targeted clientele, which s/he may need to survive, is incompatible with the hotel's clientele the hotel will suffer. Imagine a family and business oriented highway location in the suburbs with limited parking. What would happen if the food and beverage tenant targeted high-school students who tied up the restaurant tables in the early evening after extra-curriculars and sports practice? What if the operator heavily promoted an early bird al-you-can-eat buffet on Friday and Saturday nights that tied up all the parking before check-ins? Who is entitled to hotel's physical resources an one this is agreed to, how is it enforced? Why would an food and beverage tenant accept those potential restrictions on revenues?

To a hotel owner it is cash-on-cash return. It doesn't make any difference what department is making money. That information is simply used as a tool to analyze ways to improve cash flow. A food and beverage operation managed internally might have a combined departmental profit, using the Uniform System of Accounts (for hotels) of 10% - 35% of food and beverage revenues. Some expenses-accounting, marketing and maintenance for instance-are all allocated to other departments thus eroding the departmental margin. However, the reverse is also true, there is no accurate way to measure how much additional rooms revenue, the crucial element in a hotel's financial success, a well-managed food and beverage operation contributed or, at worst, did not detract from!

CONTROLLING FOOD AND BEVERAGE REVENUES

There are many reasons why hotel Food and Beverage profits are not what we would like them to be. Foremost among them is usually the fact that revenues are not as high as they might be. The lack of separate identity and entrances for outlets has a negative impact but for the most part hoteliers aren't the street fighting promoters our free standing restaurant counterparts are. This is quite understandable, after all why should we focus so heavily on Food and Beverage when for the time and money spent it will never be as profitable as the Rooms Division!

There are some subtle differences that make a lot of sense. Think about how you'd spend your finite promotional dollars if you had a choice between promoting the hotel in its entirety or just a profitable restaurant outlet. Clearly it makes more sense to advertise the hotel and its services or to have the sales staff either build commercial room demand or pursue group room bookings. These items have profit margins in excess of 75 - 80%.

A hotel's Food and Beverage department is an exception if profit exceeds 20%. In both cases as hoteliers must admit, administrative, marketing, maintenance and utilities expenses are not deductions from these margins. Unlike our restaurant counterparts who must bear all these expenses directly we shuffle them off as Unallocated Expenses. In the end it makes sense because most hotel Food and Beverage revenues are driven by the Rooms Department's level of activity and our buildings and operational structures are not such that some expenses can be isolated cost effectively. Can you imagine the time required to allocate the credit card commission expenses for Food and Beverage charged to the guest rooms from those having to do with the Telephone Department and room sales?

So what do we think the answer is to Food and Beverage profitability in a hotel environment? Increase hotel guest usage, increase hotel guest average checks, and increase outside patronage from the community. You say those things are obvious but do you have a mini-business plan for each of your Food and Beverage outlets? Does it address those items? Is it funded, are all the departments' employees involved and excited about it? Are the key players motivated with incentives to make the plans succeed?

Mini-business plan? You know, like the one you have for the hotel; revenue and expense goals in detail, staffing plan, capital budget, menu plan and outlet market plan. These are not all new things, everything but the menu plan and outlet market plan should be in your hotel's annual business plan, so preparing a mini-plan for each Food and Beverage outlet should not be a monumental task.

We refer to these plans as mini-plans because they can be three small lists: standard hotel procedures, one time promotions and advertising. Standard hotel procedures are simple things like having the reception staff mention the outlets to registering guests and having the bell staff mention that night's restaurant specials while the guest is a captive audience. Hyatt has a promotion titled something like, "The Winner is...". Its based on the envelope they open for the Academy Awards and is a small folded over card which the server opens and entitles the guest to anything from a 10% to

50% discount on dinner. These cards are handed out by the receptionist registering the guest.

Other standard items are elevator displays, in room promotions, and promotional cards given with restaurant and bar checks. Why not room service sales messages adjacent to the emergency telephones at the swimming pool? One hotel we work with in Denver promotes its seafood buffet with a tasteful fish- shaped card stock flyer hanging on the guest room shower heads for arriving guests. Nobody misses seeing it and reading it!

Standard hotel procedures must include services, attitudes and amenities that are very appealing to the hotel's guests. Services are kind of obvious but attitudes are a little tougher. Rather than exclusively hiring experienced servers look for people with a positive, cheerful outgoing attitude that either have experience or are trainable. A cheerful good attitude will over-come a lot of service and even quality problems, assuming they are short term! Your servers must enjoy their patrons, thank them for coming, ask them if they will be in tomorrow, how their room is, etc. In short they must care. It will help the food and Beverage outlets and the hotel in general.

Amenities are a more exciting and creative issue. Sure there should be an assortment of newspapers at breakfast and with room service. But what about a heated pot of coffee so that the patrons don't have to wait to be bothered by, "...more coffee?" every few minutes. Can you promote your restaurant or coffee shop as the area's power breakfast meeting place? Offer cut fruit with every order for the health conscious and thick slab bacon or what ever is locally popular for the heavy eaters. Why not free shoe shines as patrons leave and for people waiting for a table or for joiners? Dare to be different and work hard to find out what your hotel guests and surrounding community want. Who eats at Perkins and Bakers Square and why? What is so good and unique about them that can't be copied?

Advertising for food and beverage outlets ranges from the basics like the Yellow Pages and entertainment directories to such media as radio and television. Any media that can be obtained for free is good as long as one has some control over it. Trade outs are always a good idea. The best trade a Food and Beverage manager can arrange is rooms for advertising! Next to that, beverage for advertising is good if it can be obtained on some multiple like four advertising dollars for one beverage dollar. Doing joint promotions with media outlets is especially effective if one can obtain extra advertising unrelated to the promotion at a later time in order to stay in the audience's mind.

Never forget the power of good press releases. These should be done for all conventions, banquets, menu changes, new entertainment, etc. Invite the press in to try new menus and to witness promotions. Charities are good tie ins. In an Econo Lodge we manage we have a Charity of the Month where we donate 1% of the hotel's revenues to charity. For the past two months it has been the Shriners Hospital and for the next few months it will be various parts of the Athletic Department at the University of Minnesota. A similar program at a hotel restaurant will raise the outlet's profile in the community over time and accomplish worthwhile things. There are obviously direct benefits if the charity is selected wisely.

As a final point let us emphasize the value of employee involvement. They should be involved in brainstorming sessions to create ideas in every area affecting revenues and expense control. They know more about the customers and the operations than management and owners do. More importantly when they have bought into the promotional ideas they will be good at delivering the product and service to the patrons but also at going out and promoting it.

Significant long-term increases in Food and Beverage revenues can only be achieved with the staff's enthusiastic understanding and support. And that's not limited to Food and Beverage Division employees; Rooms Division employees may be the only employees to have any contact with your in-house guests during their stay if you don't get them into the outlets.

Growth in Rates

The ability of hotels to raise their room rates three to four times the pace of inflation has certainly been a major contributing factor to the record levels of profitability achieved by the hotel industry in the 1990s. However, hotels and motels were not the only forms of lodging to enjoy strong growth in rates. In fact, beds breakfast and bucks (B&Bs)and country inns not only achieve higher average room rates than their respective comparable hotel categories, but their ADRs have grown at a faster pace since 1996.

In USA, in 1998, the average B&B achieved an ADR of $121.75, 11.7 percent greater than the ADR in 1996. This compares to an ADR for limited-service hotels of $58.91 and a growth rate of 11.1 percent. Comparing properties with food and beverage, the ADR for Country Inns was $133.84 in 1998, compared to $107.68 for full-service hotels. Again, since 1996, rate growth has been greater for country inns (20.1 percent) than full-service hotels (15.6 percent).

Comparative Occupancy and Average Room Rate

	Bed and Breakfast	Limited -Service	Country Inn	Full Service
Occupancy	50.0%	66.3%	39.0%	70.3%
ADR	$121.75	$58.91	$133.84	$107.68

Prime Guests

Separate surveys have found that the typical B&B/ Country Inn guest is relatively affluent and well educated. Not only is this exemplified in the ability to pay higher room rates, but the methods used to book their reservations. In 1998, an estimated 22 percent of bed-and-breakfast guests, and 12 percent of country inn guests used the internet to make their reservation. For newer inns (less than 4 years old), this number soars to 32 percent.

Loyalty is also a trait among inn guests. On average, 17 percent of B&B guests and 22 percent of country inn guests have previously stayed at the inn. Word of mouth is also a strong generator of demand. An average of 12 percent of B&B guests and 18 percent of country inn guests heard about the inn they chose from a former guest.

While tourists make up the largest segment of demand for inns, meeting attendees and business travelers are beginning to seek these more intimate accommodations. To appeal to these segments, more inns are adding meeting rooms. In 1998, 36 percent of all B&Bs had at least one meeting room, up from 29 percent in 1996. Given their catering capabilities, meeting rooms are much more prevalent among country inns. More than half (57 percent) of all country inns in the survey offer meeting rooms, up from 48 percent in 1996.

Mix of Guests By Purpose of Travel

	Business	Leisure	Meetings	Other
Bed & Breakfast	11%	80%	9%	0%
Limited Service	42%	49%	5%	4%
Country Inn	13%	77%	10%	0%
Full Service	40%	30%	26%	4%

Like hotels, inns have found the need to offer practical amenities to attract business travelers. In 1998, approximately 71 percent of all inns offered fax machines, up from 65 percent in 1996. Internet access is also becoming more common. Nearly 35 of all inns have internet access available on site, while an additional 12 percent have internet access available in their guest rooms.

Breakfast

For the population at large, they say breakfast is the most important meal of the day. For inns, breakfast is a defining competitive feature. Given this importance, it is not surprising that inns outspend their hotel counterparts on their complimentary breakfast offerings. The average bed-and-breakfast spends $4.22 per-occupied-room on foods for the morning meal, compared to $1.39 for limited-service hotels. The average food cost for breakfast at country inns is $4.03 per-occupied-room, while all-suite hotels that provide complimentary breakfast spend an average of $3.10.

Complimentary Breakfast Expenditures
(Dollars Per Occupied Room)

Bed and Breakfast	$4.22
Country Inn	$4.03
All-Suite	$3.10
Limited Service	$1.39

What will you find on the breakfast table? Fruit, juice, and baked goods are served by over 90 percent of bed-and-breakfast inns, followed in popularity by cheese or egg entrees, pancakes/waffles, breakfast meats, and cereal.

Breakfast Items (Percent of B&Bs Offering)

Fruit	99%
Juice	98%
Baked Goods	97%
Cheese or Egg Entree	90%
Pancakes / Waffles	87%
Meat	76%
Cereal	75%
Yogurt	57%
Regional Dishes	39%

Prime Profits

Due mainly to their small size (average 7.4 rooms), the financial performance of bed-and-breakfasts is actually superior to the average limited-service hotel when measured on a per-available-room basis. In 1998, the typical B&B averaged $6,875 per-available-room in operating profits compared to $5,600 for the average limited-service hotel. It should be noted that the B&B profit figure is before a deduction of an owner's draw.

For country inns, the comparison is reversed. The average country inn achieved an operating profit equivalent to $6,834 per-available-room, under the $12,136 figure posted by full-service hotels.

Comparative Revenues and Profits

	B&B's	Limited Service	Country Inns	Full Service
Total Revenue	$19,906	$14,953	$30,689	$42,729
Operating Profit	$6,875	$5,600	$6,834	$12,136

When evaluating the relatively profitability of inns and hotels, it should be noted that the "pay back" for innkeepers usually differs than that for the typical hotel owner. Innkeepers frequently rely upon the inn operation to pay for a portion of their housing, food, telephone, and transportation. In fact, half of all B&B owners and 30 percent of all country innkeepers still need to rely on income from other sources in order to sustain their desired lifestyle.

Comparative Profit Margins
Percent of Total Revenue B&B's 31.1%

Limited Service	37.5%
Country Inns	22.3%
Full Service	28.4%

The business of innkeeping is schizophrenic. On one hand, innkeepers are owners who need to worry about mortgage payments, property values, and income taxes. On the other hand, they are operators who need to prepare good food, manage employees, and maintain a clean and safe facility. Even though the total dollar amounts are lower than most hotel operations, the responsibilities and challenges for the owners of the nation's bed-and-breakfast and country inns are certainly equal, if not greater.

The 1998 Industry Study covered the performance of 289 bed-and-breakfast inns and 44 country inns. Country inns differ from breakfast-and-breakfasts (B&Bs) in that they serve meals other than breakfast. The study covers a wide range of operating statistics including amenities, marketing techniques, payroll costs, occupancy, room rates, financial performance, and a profile of inn owners. For a complete copy of the 1998 Industry Study of Bed-and-Breakfast and Country Inns, please contact the Professional Association of Innkeepers International at (805) 569-1853.

New Trends

We have factored in our hunches about technology, the legislative environment and the microclimates within our culture to arrive at some trends which dominate menu development recently. They are:

— *Bolder Flavors*: While the heat is still on the rise, fullness of flavor has overtaken macho levels of spice. The search for bold, intense flavors has expanded the range of the chile peppers in every chef's vocabulary. We'll see techniques which layer the flavors to make them last longer. Complex undertones will become more common, with and without spicy heat. This trend plays off of Caribbean, Latin and authentic Mexican flavors.

— *Portable Foods*: Time starved consumers are increasingly eating in their cars or at their desks, making to-go foods essential. We'll see more dripless hand-held foods and one-bowl, spoon-included to-go packets. The line will blur between nutrient-packed beverages and breakfast/lunch.

— *Don't-Call-It-Healthy Food*: For frequent restaurant diners, the words 'fresh' and 'natural' imply it will taste good while 'healthy' does not. Savvy consumers know how to find 'week-day moderation' without the label. The counter-trend is 'week-end splurges', with a stable, high market share.

— *Oasis of Calm:* There is much talk about the nostalgia for slow cooked foods and the restful comfort of good service - both difficult things for restaurants to provide in a tight labor market. Fortunately, there are more and far better value-added foodservice products being introduced - fully cooked pot roasts and meat loaves; par-baked breads in dozens of shapes and sizes. More 'signature-ready' products will be offered, with the drudgery taken care of at the factory to leave chefs time to finish the flavor in their kitchens. Watch for some QSRs to move to 'limited service', in which customers queue to order but sit and chat while servers bring their freshly cooked food.

— *Regionalization/Globalization* – Pasta consumption has doubled since the 1980s, and it is now considered to be American food, eaten 1 to 3 times per week. This means that Italian restaurants have had to dig deeper into Italian regions to maintain diners' interest. And just as Italian restaurants are now Tuscan or Venetian, Mexican restaurants will specialize in foods of the Yucatán or Oaxaca. Menu generalists go global instead, picking new flavor destinations. Look for extensive flavor mining in Southeast Asia. Indian food will continue to be treated gingerly, avoiding the use of the word 'curry'.

— *Mediterranean Spread* : A second response to the long focus on Italian food has been to include more of the Mediterranean. The specific flavors of Greece, Turkey, Spain, Portugal and North Africa, similar to Italy in their use of garlic, olive oil and seafood, and sharing the same 'healthy' aura, are only beginning to be explored. Watch for descriptions to emphasize the Italian-like elements and downplay the unfamiliar.

3

Management Priorities

The scope of a foodservice facility design project influences the design approach taken by the owner or manager. If the project involves only the layout of a new hot food production area for an existing restaurant, the approach used and the planning process will be fairly simple. If the project entails the construction of a new restaurant or the complete renovation of an existing facility, the planning process becomes more difficult. And if the project includes the construction of a new facility that is to serve as the prototype for a chain or franchise, the planning process is even more complex.

Scope can be divided into four levels of complexity, each of which requires the involvement of different individuals and different amounts of planning time. Determining the scope of the project is an important first step before the planning begins.

Projects of level I scope involve no more than the selection of a major piece of equipment or the replacement of a small area of a foodservice facility. Examples of level I projects include:

— Replacement of a dish machine and dish tables in a school cafeteria

— Replacement of the display refrigerator and service counter in a delicatessen

— Purchase and installation of an outdoor walk-in freezer in a nursing home

— Replacement of the range section in a country club

Projects of level I scope typically can be carried out under the leadership of the owner or manager, assuming that he or she is familiar with foodservice equipment and has a good grasp of the workings of the food facility. If the owner does not have a working knowledge of equipment, a food facilities design consultant may be needed. The owner also will require the assistance of the kitchen equipment dealer and/or manufacturer's representatives in selecting and installing the equipment.

Level II scope projects involve the renovation of a significant portion of an existing foodservice facility. Examples of level II scope projects include:

— Renovation of the entire service area in a university foodservice facility

— Replacement of all of the walk-in coolers and freezers in a country club

— Replacement and relocation of the warewashing system in a hospital

— Addition of banquet rooms and serving kitchens in a hotel

The professionals likely to be involved in level II scope projects include the owner, an architect, mechanical and electrical engineers, a foodservice facility design consultant, and a kitchen equipment contractor. A full complement of professionals is necessary at level II because such projects are complex and require expertise in construction, engineering, and foodservice equipment layout and design.

Level II scope projects require a much longer time to complete than do level I projects. Table 1 shows a typical time line for a level II renovation project.

Table 1: Time lines for projects of different levels of scope

Task	Level I	Level II	Level III	Level IV
Planning	1 week	4 weeks	6 weeks	3 months
Equipment Selection	1 week	2 weeks	1 month	2 months
Design and Engineering	1 week	4 weeks	2 months	4 months
Preparing Bid Documents	2 days	4 weeks	2 months	2 months
Equipment Delivery	4–6 weeks	2–3 months	4–6 months	4–6 months
Installation	3–5 days	2–6 weeks	1–3 months	1–3 months

Level III scope projects involve the complete renovation of an existing foodservice facility or the design and construction of a new foodservice facility. Examples of level III scope projects include:

— Renovation of the dietary department of a hospital

— Construction of a new theme restaurant

— Renovation of the kitchen, service, and dining areas in a country club

— The development of foodservices for a new hotel

The planning process for the renovation of a foodservice facility often is even more complex than designing a new facility because of the difficulty of dealing with existing walls, structural members, utilities, and space, and the demolition of parts of the existing structure. Moreover, in renovation projects decisions must be made about which pieces of existing equipment should or could be used in the newly renovated facility.

The professionals likely to be involved in level III scope projects include the owner, an architect, mechanical and electrical engineers, a foodservice facility design consultant, an interior designer, a general contractor, and a kitchen equipment contractor. Level III scope projects may take from one to three years from design to completion. Table 1 shows a typical time line for a level III renovation project.

Level IV scope projects involve the development of a chain or franchise prototype.Chain or prototype foodservice facilities require intense planning and design efforts because they will be constructed in multiple locations. Inefficiencies in design or inadequacies in equipment could be repeated hundreds of times, and thus will be exceptionally expensive to correct. Such projects, in addition to the requirements of level III scope projects, involve a corporate strategy, a well-researched marketing plan, complex financial planning, and a strong management team.

The food facility design at level IV must fit the needs of the menu, market, strategy, and financial package that is being developed by the corporation. Professionals likely to be involved in level IV projects include investors and/or owners of the corporation, marketing consultants, financial planners, bankers, and corporate staff specialists as well as the design team, consisting of an architect, engineers, a foodservice design consultant, an interior designer, and contractors.

The time required for a level IV scope project is longer than for a level III project in the design phases but may be shorter in the construction phases. Table 1 shows the typical amount of time required for level IV scope projects. Once the scope has been determined, the owner can move forward with the project. In level I and level II scope projects, moving forward means going directly to the design process. However, when the scope of the project involves the renovation of an existing facility or the development and construction of a new foodservice facility, the next step in the process is concept development.

Concept of Foodservice Operation Development

The concept of a foodservice operation is the overall plan for how it will meet the needs and expectations of its intended market. A foodservice operation's concept is expressed in many ways, including its menu, decor, form of service, pricing, and location. Concept development means developing a plan for the success of the operation in its market in advance of actually designing- let alone buildingthe facility.

It is not unusual for a person to consider a new restaurant or, in fact, to open a new restaurant without knowing what type of food facility will have the best chance of succeeding. The potential entrepreneur may have some investment money, a location or a theme in mind, and a great amount of enthusiasm for the food business, but has not really thought through the total concept of the operation. Unfortunately, enthusiasm and great food products are only half of the success equation. The other half of the equation is the market.

Concept development precedes the actual design of a foodservice facility because the foodservice design team must know what the menu, demand, hours of operation, and mode of service will be. The client who most frequently comes to the food facilities design consultant for help with concept development is the individual restaurant owner. The restaurant owner typically organizes a corporation comprised of a small number of local businesspeople and then begins to develop a concept that will eventually become a freestanding restaurant. The success or failure of the venture often depends on how well the concept was planned and how well the plan was followed.

Numerous concepts are possible for singleunit restaurants. Commonly found concepts often are described in terms of the following general categories:

— *Fine-dining restaurants*: Fine-dining restaurants are distinguished by fine cuisine prepared by celebrity chefs, attentive service, stylish decor, and high prices.

— *Theme restaurants*: Theme restaurants offer a dining experience that evokes special times, places, or events, such as English pubs, restaurants owned by sports celebrities, and recreations of diners from the 1950s.

— *Casual dinner houses*: Casual dinner houses emphasize a comfortable and contemporary decor, as well as high value.

— *Ethnic restaurants*: Ethnic restaurants are closely tied to the cultures or foodways from which they originated. They include Mexican, Italian, French, German, Thai, and Indian restaurants, to name but a few.

— *Family restaurants*: Family restaurants specialize in relatively inexpensive fare and are kidfriendly.

— *Quick-service restaurants*: Quick-service restaurants specialize in convenience and fast service and include fast-food operations as well as delis, bagel shops, and sandwich shops.

Each of these categories of foodservice concept involves differences in menu, decor, mode of service, and price. However, not all of these factors are equally important within a given concept. Price is a critical factor in the success of quick-service, family, and casual dinner restaurants, where customers are value-conscious.

However, price may not be as important in fine-dining restaurants, where customers expect to pay top dollar. Similarly, location is crucial for quick-service restaurants because their clientele depend upon convenient access. But for some fine-dining and theme restaurants, location is not critical. Concept development for a single-unit restaurant is thus a complex process.

Multiunit casual dinner houses and theme restaurants, such as Chili's, Bennigan's, and the Olive Garden, follow a similar pattern in concept development. Their emphasis is on identifying the key characteristics of their target markets and then locating restaurants where there is a high concentration of individuals who have those characteristics. Key characteristics may include income, age, education, and home ownership. What gives multiunit restaurants a competitive advantage over single-unit restaurants is the opportunity to learn from experience with multiple examples of the same concept.

When a chain restaurant firm has five hundred virtually identical restaurants, it can analyze the factors that differentiate its high-performing restaurants from its low-performing restaurants, and make changes as necessary before opening additional units.

A particular form of multiunit restaurant for which concept development is critical to success is the restaurant organization that opens and operates restaurants whose concepts are not identical but different.

The development of foodservice concepts for hotels has evolved in recent years from the traditional view that considered the food and beverage department as a necessary evil to the modern idea that the food and beverage department is an important profit center. Some large hotels have food and beverage sales of over $35 million per year, an amount that exceeds room sales and creates in management a high expectation of profit from these two departments.

The Hilton Hotel in Atlanta, Georgia, has developed a concept for its first-class rooftop restaurant that goes beyond the idea of a foodservice facility as a profit center. The restaurant, called Nikolai's Roof, was conceived as a luxury dining room and is marketed to the city of Atlanta as well as to hotel guests. The decor is exquisite, the food is served with flair and showmanship, and the entire theme captures the imagination of the city's residents.

The concept was developed with such success that the hotel's own guests had great difficulty getting reservations to dine. A hotel restaurant so overcrowded that it could not serve the guests of the hotel would have been unthinkable in earlier days of hotel keeping in the United States. Nikolai's Roof is an excellent example of the execution of a hotel dining concept that complements the hotel itself as well as drawing a significant number of guests from the community.

Hotel managers have known for many years that hotel restaurants must have certain desirable features if they are to be successful. These features include:

— Availability of parking

— Unique theme or decor (differing from the decor of the hotel itself)

— Strong promotion to the community

— A menu and a method of service that are distinctive

The developers of hotel properties, and in some cases hotel chains, have used outside foodservice facilities and interior design consultants to create unique specialty restaurants that can be successfully marketed to both hotel guests and the community.

Institutional foodservice is usually conceived as a service to an organization, and most often has a not-for-profit philosophy. Most institutional food operations are expected to break even, and all are expected to budget and operate within well-defined ranges of costs so that they do not become a financial burden on the organization they serve. In some cases, the institutional food operation is expected to make a profit and to pay for all of its direct and indirect operational costs.

The development of an operational concept for the institution is often ignored, and this is usually a serious mistake. The institution must accurately interpret its market and must "sell" its products, even when the food is indirectly paid for by the customer. For instance, in hospital foodservice, an unattractive meal presentation will cause dissatisfaction and complaining on the part of the patient and possibly adverse health effects as well if he or she does not eat a meal and thus does not get sufficient nourishment.

In a college or university dining hall, a comprehensive concept of service and decor can greatly influence financial success. Attractive food court service or a scramble design, for example, can increase the popularity of a college foodservice operation and generate additional profit. A dining facility operated by a corporation for its employees should also have a well-planned concept and decor. The ability of corporate foodservice operations to attract employees may influence the degree of subsidy that a company is willing to contribute to the operation.

The successful foodservice operation combines the following elements of concept development: market, menu, money, management, and method of execution (Figure 1).

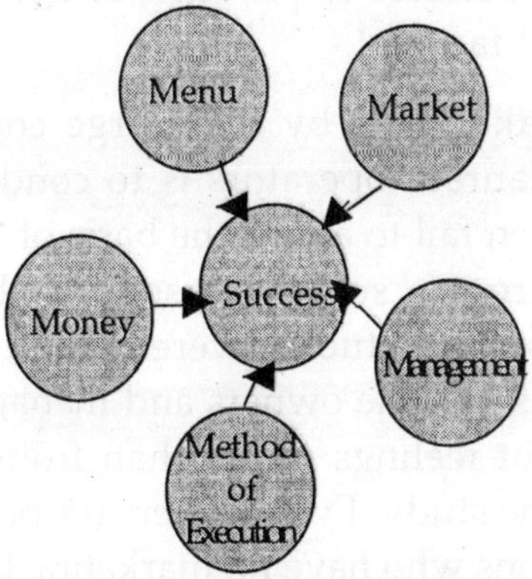

Figure 1: The five M's of concept development.

Market Analysis

The importance of conducting market studies before proceeding with the construction of a food facility cannot be too heavily stressed. The basic marketing questions that must be answered are:

— To whom is the food operation being marketed?

— Is the market large enough to generate sales and produce a profit?

— How will the market be identified?

— What method will be used to communicate to this market?

- Will the potential customer want or need the food product?
- Will a quality assurance plan be developed that will encourage the customer to return because of superior service and/or product quality?
- Will internal marketing successfully sell the customer additional services or products after he or she arrives at the food facility?

A classic mistake made by both large corporations and individual restaurant operators is to conduct the market analysis and then fail to act on the basis of the information obtained. There are several cases in which extensive marketing feasibility studies were conducted by outside marketing firms, but the owners and managers made their decisions on gut feelings rather than from the hard data derived from the study. Even owners (or potential owners) of food operations who have no marketing background can conduct their own market research, with a small amount of guidance and a large amount of energy and common sense.

The importance of the menu to the design of the food facility cannot be overemphasized. The subject of menu writing is too broad to be addressed adequately in a book on foodservice facilities design. The owner or manager is encouraged to seek additional sources of information as a part of the process of developing a menu for a new or renovated food operation. The menu has a tremendous influence on the design and success of a food operation. From a design and layout perspective, these are just some of the factors determined by the menu:

- *Amount of space required*: A complex menu requires more space to prepare than a limited or simple menu does, because separate work-stations and additional equipment are necessary.

— *Service area size and design*: The greater the number of menu items, the more area required for service. For example, in a cafeteria each beverage requires a dispenser and each entree a point of service.

— *Dishwashing area size and dish machine capacity*: Complex menus often require multiple plates, dishes, and utensils, and so the dishwashing area and machine capacity will need to be greater than in the case of simple menus.

— *Types of cooking equipment*: Complex menus require multiple types of equipment, especially in the final preparation area, where it may be necessary to steam, fry, bake, broil, and sauté.

— *Equipment capacity*: Limited menus may require relatively few pieces of equipment but need large capacities of each. Complex menus may require many different types of equipment with relatively small capacities.

— *Size of dry and refrigerated storage areas*: Complex menus may require larger storage areas to maintain the par stocks necessary to meet demand.

— *Number of employees*: Simple menus require fewer employees than do complex menus.

— *Amount of investment required*: When large or complex menus require more equipment, space, and employees, costs rise.

Successful capitalization of a food facility includes funds for:

— Planning costs

— Building construction or renovation

— Equipment (fixed)

— China, glassware, utensils

— Furniture and fixtures

— Decor

— Operating costs

These funds must be identified and committed before serious planning can begin. Yet, in concept development, the commitments may not be made in the early planning stage because the costs are not yet known. Therefore, planning for capital funds is a two-step process: First the financial needs are estimated and sources of financial support are contacted to determine the possibility of obtaining investment funds; then, after concept development has taken place, preliminary designs and construction estimates have been made, and market research is completed, financial commitments are made by lenders and investors.

The industry experts have long sought to establish the right 'pedigree' of menu analysis for foodservice operators and educational guidelines. Currently, there are plenty of theoretical alternative approaches to menu analysis available published in professional hospitality journals. Although all of these menu analysis approaches advocate different tactical solutions for analyzing the menu items, performance, they all share the same objective, which to improve (or to provide a solution for) the current menu items performance.

However the question that poses a great dilemma for the foodservice operators is which approaches or methods are suitable for practical application? A recent research indicates that none of the theoretical approaches of menu analysis is totally embraced by the foodservice operators when a menu analysis is conducted.

Menu is one of the important aspects for the success of any foodservice establishment. Perhaps it is arguably the soul of the restaurant. Menu infers several interpretations for both the buyers and sellers. Khan suggests that "menus are statements" of the food and-beverage items provided by a foodservice establishment, primarily based on consumer needs and/or demands and designed to achieve organisational objectives".

Mooney and Kreck note that menu can be interpreted as a list of product range that a restaurant offers and the same time it can be a piece of literature or display used to communicate the product range to the customer. However, a recent study argues that "menus are more than the conventional function of a communications and selling tool but also a research and experimentation device that can be studied to increase restaurant profit".

An interesting point is that the battle for pre-eminence menu offered to the consumers is an endless task faced by most foodservice operators. The model of new menu development advocated by Mooney which is illustrated in Figure 2, shows how critical it is to have thorough research and analysis of the various elements from the restaurant's objectives and strategies to the bureaucratic processes of menu planning, selection, design, pricing and analysis.

A matter of fact this process is actually an endless cycle of research and analysis because once a new menu is developed that menu is periodically reviewed for its effectiveness. Quite simply, the research process is crucial to find out what is going on in the market and the analysis process determines which dishes need further assessment.

Figure 2. Model of New Menu Development

Marketing Objective >>>	Service objectives and strategy	<<< Environmental analysis
Internal sources >>>	Idea generation and screening	<<< Magazines / competitors /etc.
Budget development >>>	Menu framework development	
Dish cost development >>>	Menu item screening	<<< Market assessment
Yield testing >>>	Menu item design and testing	<<< Consumer taste panel
Opertional personel >>>	Operational testing	
	Market testing launch new menu	<<< Consumers <<< Consumers
Menu analysis >>>	Review menu effectiveness	

In broad terms, menu analysis can be defined as a range of techniques and procedures that enable more effective decision making both with respect to marketing and operating the menu. Various tactical solutions to menu analysis have been sought in endless attempts by many restaurant operators to improve menu perfor-mance. One of the notable approaches that has gained enormous momentum both from the hospitality literature and educational curriculum is Boston's matrix technique also known as the 'portfolio analysis' or menu engineering'. Jones defines this approach as the "systematic evaluation of a menu's cost and/or sales data for the purpose of identifying opportunities for improved performance".

One of the specific Boston's matrix techniques known as menu engineering made popular by Kasavana and Smith has taken a step further with the introduction of the computer software packages. However, the irony is many scholars and menu planners have criticized the imperfection of these matrix approaches including the Kasavana and Smith's menu engineering approach.

Subsequently more tactical solutions to menu analysis have emerged. The issue of non-material variable costs, which is claimed being ignored in the previous menu analysis approaches, becomes prevalent of its important in the works of Hayes and Huffman, Bayou and Bennett and LeBruto et. al. respectively. Other approaches such as the micro-marketing mix and economic approach have each advocated their own method of tactical solutions to menu analysis.

Although all these menu analysis approaches advocate different tactical solutions for analysing the menu items' performance, they all share the same objective, which to improve (or to provide a solution for) the current menu items performance. However, the question that poses a great dilemma for the foodservice operators is which approaches or methods are suitable for practical applications?

Recent research indicates that menu analysis is not purely on the "process of analysing costs and sales data in order to manipulate.. products on the menu [but understand] in-depth customers' need and perceptions". A recent survey conducted by HOTELS reveals that there are alternative approaches to menu analysis that can build revenue and keep repeat customers. According to the survey, the positioning and descriptions of the menu item on the menu can influence its popularity. In addition the survey also points out that creative menu design with the use of tasteful product pictures and the size of the menu are an integral part of menu planners' menu analysis. The summary reveals that there is no definite evidence of what actual/or dominant method(s) of menu analysis are adopted by menu planners in the global foodservice industry. The industry experts have long sought to establish the right "pedigree" of menu analysis for the foodservice operators and educational guidelines. In order to achieve this, further research is required to examine and understand how menu analysis is conducted by menu planners.

Menu Analysis: Qualitative Approach

A research on menu analysis conducted in UK, a qualitative approach was undertaken to ascertain chain foodservice attitudes in the menu analysis decision-making. Although the acceptance of qualitative research methodology was less prevalent than the quantitative research, was argued that the choice of qualitative research would fulfil the needs of the purpose of the research project. The interest of the research was a phenomenological approach, an approach to understanding how menu analysis is conducted by foodservice operators rather than the use of a positivist approach, which is largely based on measurable variables and provable propositions.

The qualitative research approach to inquiry also involved a case study approach, where people and setting were explored in-depth and described in a series of mini-case studies reports. It is believed that a series of mini case studies reports would enhance the body of knowledge in understanding the intended research objectives. Thus, personal interviews were deployed to explore the phenomenon of interest from the foodservice operators with the use of a semi-structured questionnaire, which was composed based on the secondary research and piloted in predetermined sampling settings.

Undoubtedly, a large-scale population would make the qualitative case study research more valid and reliable. However, to conduct in-depth personal interviews in a large-scale survey would be too costly and time consuming. This to a large extent answers why a case study approach was adopted in the qualitative research.

A list of twelve UK chains companies with over 25 restaurants brands was compiled. The reason behind the selection of chain restaurants was as followed: Restaurants that have a chain affiliation are known to be more standardised and organised in their overall operations.

Mass financial capabilities and diversification of divisions and departments provide huge advantage in making the operations more efficient and effective. Furthermore with the increased numbers of outlets, a need for better menu analysis methodology is surely crucial apart from being competitive in the market.

To a large extent, the variables that needed to be measured were quite complex and subjective because most of the different approaches to menu analysis advocated different criteria and each of them function differently. Some of the menu analysis approaches have incorporated tangible and intangible elements to advocate their menu analysis techniques. Because of this, 'statistical generalization' or enumerate frequencies' were considered unsuitable, instead 'analytical generalisation' or 'expand and generalise theories' was a more appropriate selection of measurement.

Table 2. Major UK Chain Restaurants, 1994-1995

Company	Key Brands	Outlets
Allied Domecq	Big Steak, Wacky Warehouse, Exchange	270
Bass	Toby, Harvester	278
Bright Reason PLC	Pizzaland, Bella Pasta, Pizza Piazza	190
City Centr Rest. PLC	Deep Pan Pizza, Garfunkels, Chiuita, Caffe Uno, UK Diner, Raja Mama's, Nachos	205
Granada	Happy Eater, Little Chef, Welcome Break, Granada	400
Grand Metropolitan	Burger King	380
McDonald's	McDonald's	650
Pelican	Cafe Rouge, Dome	100
Pepsico	KFC	367
Pizza Express	Pizza Express	94
Scottish & Newcastle	Chef & Brewer, Old Orleans	1,600
Whitbread	Beeffeater, T.G.I Friday's, Pizza Hut, Brewer Fayne	875

According the research findings, the obvious equipment used by the chain operators to analyse the menu performance is the Electronic Point-of-Sale (EPOS). Almost all of these chain companies have an advance computer system, which is linked with the EPOS. Because of this the menu analysis is entirely conducted in the head office and such analysis from the EPOS at the restaurant outlets are no longer applicable.

Quantitative data analysis is predominantly the main method to assess the menu mix sales volume popularity) and gross profit profitability/ contribution margin). The findings imply that once the new menu is launched in the market, the first criterion used to review the menu effectiveness is the menu sales mix reports (quantitative data). Daily sales mix reports are accumulated for a period of one month to produce a monthly sales mix report. Every menu item sales volume and gross profit are analysed and the outcomes of what actions should be done for the menu items are decided in several ways.

However, the quantitative data analysis is not the sole determinant to decide what actions should be done to the menu items. Other criteria such as based on intuition, experience and company's financial policy are also taken into considerations for appropriate alternative approaches. This seems to confirm Jones's propositions where he argues that 'menu changes.. .are based on strategic decisions rather than simply on analyses of operating performance (and) the addition and removal of a new menu item is often based on competitive and market analysis"

Qualitative analysis approach is indeed equally important as the quantitative data analysis for the chain operators when a menu analysis is conducted, specifically deciding what actions should be done for the menu items. Endless research projects are carried out to analyse customer trends in food preferences and acceptances. These research projects are vital to supplement information for menu development so that improvement for new and current menu items in term of its value and nutritional acceptances, taste, ingredients and presentation can be enhanced.

The analysis of customer trends was obtained in many ways. The findings reveal that market analysis was the common method used to obtain the plausible answers of customer trends. Analysing the target market disposable income and age population, competitors menu and awareness of current issues in food preferences and acceptances is the main areas of concern in the market analysis. Apart from the market analysis, travelling to Italy and French, which known of their gastronomic expertise was visited regularly to seek popular dishes that suitable for UK market, particularly in London market.

Based on intuition and experiences rather than relying detailed quantitative analysis are also played crucial part when a menu analysis is conducted. It should be remembered that most of these chain companies have been established for many years therefore, decision on how to analyse, amend and develop the menu items is largely based on previous experiences. Because of this, many of the chain operators analyse their menu items by advertised its on the black board menu, popular radio channels, and relevant magazines.

Customer feedback such as complaints, suggestions and compliments about the menu items are crucial for the success of the menu efficiency. Sometimes low popularity and profitability of menu items may not cause by diminishing of customer demands but poor control of the food production is likely be the culprit.

Because of this, mystery shoppers are assigned to analyse the menu performances in term of its quality, presentation, taste, and the waiting period after the order taken. The accumulative of the crucial information is indeed the 'source of aspirations' for the chain operators to act what amendments and developments should be done for the menu items.

The findings appear to disclose that the prevalent methods of how menu analysis is conducted by chain operators are combination of qualitative and quantitative analyses. These findings can be linked to Mooney's model of new menu development, where he argues that the review of menu effectiveness is performed after all the menu development processes are thoroughly analysed and implemented.

Review of Menu Effectiveness

Notably, quantitative data analysis is the dominant approach used by chain foodservice operators when analysing the menu mix. The use of sales mix reports generated by EPOS is the main source of inputs to analyse the menu mix performances. Sales volume popularity) and gross profit profitability / contribution margin) are the common criteria under investigation for every menu item. In addition, the use of gross profit percentage (GPP) is also found to be adopted.

Although different methods are used to measure menu effectiveness, some of the methodologies used by the chain operators to analyse the menu item popularity and profitability seem corroborated with the theoretical menu analysis approaches. Nevertheless, none of the theoretical methodologies of menu analysis are totally embraced by the chain operators.

Apart from using the quantitative data to analyse the menu performances, the use of mystery shoppers is also adopted to analyse the menu performances in term of its quality taste, value and overall presentation. Additionally, periodical inspection of food production processes are also conducted by the chain operators for making sure all standard procedures are followed according to specification. The finding implies that these analyses are indeed very essential so that the generation of the sales analysis produces more accurate and reliable information.

After the menu analysis is completed, the next stage is to determine whether the menu items should be modified or not. Based on the theoretical menu analysis approaches, clear guidelines of what solution should be done for the menu items are demonstrated. Unfortunately, there is no definite evidence emerged in the findings in term of which criteria used to decide whether the menu items should be modified or not. Furthermore, the decision to ascertain which alternative approaches should be taken for the menu items is somehow varied from one chain operator to another.

For example, one of the chain operators is hardly relied on the sales analysis, instead the company's President experiences in products improvement (modification) is the main source for decision-making. Unlike, other chain operator, the menu items are analysed comprehensively and it involves more than one person/department. Yet, the decision to ascertain which alternative approaches should be taken for the menu items is still pending on the market research and customer trends. Thus, the decision making to decide which appropriate approaches to be done for the menu items is quite complex and it involves various persons / departments. Nevertheless, regardless of which decision the chain operators decide to base on, several alternative approaches are highlighted based on the findings of the case studies, which can be the ideal solution. Detail explanations of each of these alternative approaches are presented below.

Alternative Approaches to Simple Menu Analysis

There are four alternative approaches, which fall under the 'simple menu analysis'.

— Promotion,

— Re-position,

— Retention and

— Elimination

are the notable findings used by the chain operators when they decided not to do anything to the menu items regardless of what results obtained from the sales analysis. It should be remembered that in the theoretical menu analysis, especially the Boston's matrix approaches, any menu items that are categorised 'problem items' will be modified its composition in order to change the items to 'star' or 'prime' category. However, in reality this is no the case. From the analysis, it is found that the main reasons why the foodservice operators are declined to modify the menu items composition are because of the following criteria:

— *Menu Promotion*: Promotion is used to analyse further the menu effectiveness because experiences and marketing strategy indicated that lack of awareness from the public eyes may be the caused why the menu items are low in demand. This strategy is adopted because the result of low popularity obtained from the sales analysis may not be necessary due to loss of customer demands. This strategy correlate with Bowen and Morris definition that highlights the advertising maxim, "unseen is unsold". Sometimes the demand of the menu items is still alive but lack of public attentions can cause the faith of the menu items in jeopardy therefore, every precaution should be observed before the menu items undergo such modifications.

Menu promotion involves both internally and externally. Black board menu and mini table standing menu, which highlights 'problem dishes' only, are the example of internal promotion. On the other hands, using popular radio channels, posters and fliers in busy places such as cinema, hybrid places, etc. is the notable findings in their external promotions.

— *Menu Repositioning*: Changing the presentation and layout of the menu design is quite essential for boosting the menu sales. A matter of fact, this is one of the dominant approaches used to boost the sales of low popularity menu items by placing them at the strategic location known to be in the centre of the menu. These findings can be linked to the works of Miller, where, according to him, menu items that most want to sell should be placed above the middle on a one-page menu.

The analysis carried out on respondents' responses has revealed that placing the items at the wrong position can cause an adverse effect of its demand. Because of this, the result of the sales analysis to some extent can provoke incorrect decision on what solutions should be taken for the menu items. Additionally, proper choice of words uses to describe the dish ingredients and methods of cooking also played a part for improving the menu popularity.

— *Menu Retention*: Undoubtedly, successful menu performances in term of its popularity and profitability should be retained. There is nothing to do with these menu items except to maintain or/and improve its quality in order to increase the popularity. However, an interesting finding obtained is that any menu items, which are known as 'problem items', are still being retained in the menu. Nonetheless, the composition of these items is subjected to be reviewed and modification is likely to be implemented.

Subsequently, once these three options are finalised and implemented, the menu items will undergo to menu analysis again. In fact, the review of menu effectiveness is an ongoing process mainly because of the changes in customer demands. It is these changes in customer demand, which make the menu items to be reviewed periodically.

Needless to say, the ultimate aim is to detect the 'shadow of customer demands' (which either be high or low) before it happened. Thus, the use of sales analysis to measure the menu effectiveness to correlate with the alternative approaches as to improve the item performance is insufficient.

A matter of fact, using market analysis and customer feedback to detect customer trends and correlates with the alternative approaches as to improve the items performance is more convincing than the sales analysis. These findings probably answer the reason why the theoretical menu, which uses hard data to analysis menu item performance as to improve the item popularity and profitability, is problematic.

— *Menu Elimination*: There are several reasons why decision is made to eliminate the menu item. Menu items that are no longer popular properly due to menu fatigue and changes of customer preferences and acceptances such as healthy foods are the real caused why the menu items are eliminated. Limited supplies and escalating in product prices are also found to be the caused for menu items to have been eliminated. An interesting point emerges that decision making to eliminate menu items is predominantly based on qualitative analysis rather than from the sales analysis.

— *Introduce New Menu Items*: Decision to introduce new menu items is mainly because of customer demands. The most common sources referred by the chain foodservice operators when considering to add menu items into the menu are company's research and development department (R&D), market information from Mintel and Keynote reports and Henley Data, professional hospitality journals and customer feedback. It should be remembered that the addition of menu items can only be materialised after thorough analysis from market demands. Moreover, current kitchen equipment and personal expertise about the new dishes are also due consideration in the internal analysis. Finally, the new menu items are launched in the market and the process of measuring the menu items effectiveness begins again.

Alternative Approaches to Complex Menu Analysis

There are five alternative approaches, which fall under the 'complex menu analysis'.

— Presentation,

— Re-price,

— Re-costing,

— Modify recipes and

— Reposition

are the notable alternative approaches used by the chain foodservice operators to modify the menu items composition. The finding reveals that most of the chain operators make the decision to modify the menu items based on the actual performance against the predetermined criteria and allow the menu items to be further developed as appropriate. In this case, menu items which fall below acceptable level are bound to be undergone such modifications. Unfortunately, details of the 'acceptable level' are somehow quite ambiguous. It appears that there is no definite time period when the menu must be changed or modified after the launched of the menu. Regardless of how frequents the menu items are modified, here are the alternative approaches adopted by chain operators as to improve the current menu items performance.

— *Menu Items Presentation*: The main references that are used to decide the modifications of the menu items presentation are mystery shoppers and the customers. Customer feedback such as complaints and suggestions are essential for improving the menu items presentation. However, what form of research instrument are used to seek customer feedback is not mentioned. The author suggests that an "informal procedure" is likely to have been adopted where such feedback is reported on a random basis based on the recollection of staff experiences.

  Unlike the mystery shoppers, there are more formal and standardised, and independently performed by outside foodservice consultant. Depending on this feedback analysis, the presentation of the menu items may be modified either one or combination of these elements: taste, garnishing, saltiness, colour, texture, etc. Nevertheless, the use of chefs artistic expertise in food presentation also plays a part in decision making for menu items presentation.

— *Menu Re-pricing:* Usually, such decision to re-price the menu items is caused by several factors. The finding indicates that inflation is the main caused why chain operators re-price the menu items. Another factor that contributed to menu re-pricing is because of over-pricing the menu items. For example, one of the operators says tha t over-pricing the menu items could be the main reason why the demand of such items declined and not because of the deterioration of the foods quality or demand. When the selling price is changed to slightly low than the former one, the popularity of the menu items has increased by 5 percents. In addition, unavoidable factors such increase in distribution costs and liquor tax imposed by the Government also lead to re-pricing the menu items. Of course, other considerations such as company financial policy, food costs and pricing strategies are also contributed to the changing of the selling price. For instance, the psychological pricing method whère by all the menu prices end with either 5 or 9 number, which can be associated with the theory of 'magic numbers or costless approaches' highlighted by Pavesic and Carvin & Norkus also found being used by these chain operators.

— *Menu Re-costing:* The cause of re-costing menu items is highly correlated with the change of the product specifications. Any changes on products purchase price from the suppliers therefore, leads to the change of the standard specifications. Notably, the standard specifications are designed by the menu planners which than becomes the control tools for menu recipes and portion size. Simply put, any modification on the items' presentation is indirectly caused its recipe specifications to change. Thus, any changes involve between these factors will lead to menu re-costing. Apart for that, the change of the item portion size also leads to menu re-costing. Above all, many chain operators have allocated a budgeted food costs by the Finance department for every chain's outlet for cost control purposes. Hence, any chains' outlets that are found to have been exceeding the budgeted food costs that outlets' menu items cost will be reviewed and menu re-costing is subsequently followed.

— *Recipes modification*: Recipe modification is basically linked with the menu re-costing.

— *Menu Re-positioning:* Unlike the menu repositioning discussed earlier, this part discusses those menu items that involve several modifications from its name, recipe, selling price and presentation. The findings reveal that after the menu items undergo several modifications (depending on how many menu items are modified) new menu design is developed with high probability of changing the menu layout and general presentation of the menu card, since the former menu card is no longer applicable with the modifications being made. Thus, the applications of the menu repositioning discussed earlier are being used again. However, if only a small proportion of the menu items undergone such modifications than the menu items may go for promotion or repositioning.

— *Launch Revised Menu Item(s):* Subsequently, after the menu items undergone such modifications regardless of which alternative approach is used these revised menu items are reviewed of its effectiveness again. Similar procedures of menu analysis discussed above are applied and the processes of how menu analysis is conducted begin again.

Managing Water Issues

There are many ways to reduce water usage in the kitchen. Traditionally, saving water has not been a major consideration of commercial food preparers. Many establishments cite the lack of money or employees as reasons for not using water conservation methods. Studies have shown that water efficiency programs are cost-effective, and most initial costs are retrieved within a two-year period. Participation in water efficiency programs shows that there is a concern for efficient water. These programs are supported by local communities.

Inefficient uses of water in kitchen operations come mainly from two areas: equipment design and behavioral patterns. The main types of water-using equipment found in kitchens are dishwashers, faucets, ice- making machines, and garbage disposal use. Improved technology has eliminated many of the water issues associated with equipment, as more rigid standards have been created to curtail excessive water use.

Water audits of commercial facilities have shown that 60 percent of identified water savings comes from simply installing faucet aerators in all kitchen sink outlets. An effective part of water savings in kitchens is attributed to behavioral patterns in facilities. Awareness programs, education, training, and job performance measures can influence proper behavioral patterns of staff.

All dishwashing machines employ wash, rinse, and sanitizing cycles. The sanitizing cycle typically is the chemical reduction of microorganisms to safe levels on any food utensil. The time taken for a dishwasher to complete a cycle is a combination of mechanical action, water temperature, and chemical action. Most dishwashers use between 2.0 and 7.0 gpm for a complete cycle of cleaning and sanitation.

Hot water use varies with the pressure of supply lines, operation speed of the machine, and dish table layout. All these variables are intrinsically linked and any adjustments affect each component. For example, rapid washing cycles necessitate stronger mechanical action and more concentrated detergents for cleaning.

There are four main types of dishwashing machines: undercounter, door, conveyor, and flight. A wide array of models and accessories are available for each category. Requirements for machine size can be calculated by estimating the amount of traffic that will be served in the food service area. Energy guidelines and water consumption levels for dishwashers are becoming stricter, and many manufacturers offer new water-saving models.

Undercounter Machines

Smallest of commercial dishwashers, undercounter dishwashers are best suited for small establishments of about 60 people. They commonly are used in nursing homes, churches, small food service areas, office buildings, and for glass washing in taverns and bars. The undercounter machines are similar to residential dishwashers in that the door opens downward with rack(s) rolling out onto the lowered door for access. A revolving wash arm handles the wash and rinse cycles, with a small holding tank being automatically drained after each cycle. An automatic timer controls cycle length.

Undercounter machines come in both hot water and chemical sanitizing models, with optional booster heaters for the latter. Undercounter machines use the most water per rack of all commercial dishwashers. This illustrates the need to wash only full racks when the machine is in use.

Door-type Machines

Manufactured to service 50-200 people, door type machines are the most widely used of commercial dishwashing machines. Door machines are used in schools, hospitals, churches, restaurants, catering businesses, fast-food establishments, and as glass and utensil units in larger operations. These box-shaped machines have singular or multiple doors that slide vertically for loading and unloading. Door type machines are available in high temperature and chemical sanitizing models. These ihdump and rinsela machines have a single tank for water and detergent, which are circulated in measured volumes and temperatures. Two revolving spray arms (one above and one below the dish rack) distribute wash solutions evenly over the dishes. Some door-type machines now have the ability to recycle rinse water to be reused in a wash cycle.

C-line Conveyor, Rack Machines

C-line, or rack conveyor, machines use a motor-driven conveyor belt to move the rack-loaded dishes through a large tank with separate wash and rinse compartments. Most widely-used in hotels, large restaurants, hospitals, schools, and universities, these machines are well suited for service of 200 or more people and accommodating most heavy food service operations.

C-line machines come in varying sizes, with available additions such as pre-wash units, side-loading trays, condensers, and blower-dryers. A single tank holds the water and detergent at a regulated temperature. The wash solution is pumped through multiple spray arms (revolving or stationary) that run constantly once the machine is operational, regardless the presence of a dish rack. The rack is then sent through the rinse compartment, where it is sprayed with the 180 F water by spray nozzles above and below the rack. C-line machines with multiple tanks differ in that some use stationary versus rotating spray arms. The racks then are sent into a pump-driven rinse tank that rinses the dishes heavily. This process usually uses recycled water from the final rinse.

All rack conveyor machines have a timer control for the speed of the conveyor to assure proper wash and rinse times. Water efficient measures, such as the installation of an electric eye sensor (that keeps the conveyor from running when there are no dishes on the racks), have started to make rack conveyors more energy- and cost-effective. Some efficient conveyors can reduce final rinse consumption from 300 gph to 130 gph. The use of energy-efficient boosters and low-flow pumps can reduce energy and water consumption levels by 50 percent.

Flight type Machines

Similar in that they use a conveyor belt to move dishware, flight type machines do not have racks. Rather, dishes are loaded directly onto the belt. Flight type dishwashers provide high-volume washing capa-bility needed only in the largest institutional, com-mercial, and industrial facilities. Variations in possible machine additions include power scrapers, power wash, power rinse, final rinse, and blower-dryers. Water efficient strategies for these machines include the recirculation of final rinse water, electric eye sensors, extra-wide conveyors, and low-energy built-in booster heaters.

The volume of consumption in dishwashers can be reduced by a variety of practices, all of which target awareness of equipment and operation needs.

Behavioral Modifications

— Educate staff about the benefits of water efficiency and the importance of hand scraping before loading a dishwasher.

— Instruct staff to quickly report leaks and troubleshoot.

— Only run rack machines if they are full.

— Try to fill each rack to maximum capacity.

Mechanical Modifications

— Recycle final rinse water for washing.

— Keep flow rates as close as possible to manufacturer specifications.

— Install inelectric eye sensorsli to allow water flow only when dishes are present.

— Install door switches for convenient on/off access.

— Check voltage of booster heater to make sure it fits the machine.

— Use issteam doorslm to prevent water loss due to evaporation.

— Install low-temperature machines that rely on chemical sanitizing over high water temperature.

— Check volume of service and estimate facility needs ¾ a better option may be a larger machine that has a lower water flow rate per rack.

Kitchen Faucets and Pre-rinse Sprayers

Faucets can waste large amounts of water, as they are the most heavily used water source in kitchens. Conventional faucets, with typical flow rates of 2.5 to 4.0 gpm, can waste as much as 40 gallons of water a day when not fully closed. Since 1994, water efficiency standards have been federally mandated, requiring that all post-1994 manufactured faucets consume a maximum of 2.5 gpm at 80psi. But many facilities have older fixtures with rubber gaskets that wear and deform because of high amounts of hot water use. By simply installing a brass gasket and an automatic shut-off nozzle, a facility could save as much as 21,000 gallons of water per year.

Many adjustments and technology advancements have been made in faucet design as a variety of low-flow faucet types are manufactured. Foot-activated kitchen faucets will reduce water use while providing additional convenience. Faucets used in kitchens will be primarily the conventional type or pre-rinse pressure sprayers. There are a variety of modifications that can be employed for all types.

Water Efficiency Options for Kitchen Faucets

— Adjust flow valve to reduce water flow.

— Check for leaks and worn gaskets.

— Install a flow restrictor to limit maximum flow rate to 2.5 gpm or less.

— Install a 2.5 gpm faucet aerator, maximizing flow efficiency by increasing airflow to the stream.

— Consider infrared or ultrasonic sensors that activate water flow only in the presence of hands or some other object.

— Install pedal operated faucet controllers to ensure valves are closed when not in use.

— Educate staff to look for leaks and broken faucets in their area.

— Do not leave faucets on to thaw vegetables and other frozen foods.

— Post water conservation literature and reminders to staff around work areas.

Pre-rinse Sprayers

Pre-rinse sprayers are used for rinsing cooking utensils, pots, pans, soaking dishes, and cleaning. They are designed with automatic shut-off valves at the hose head to supply water only when needed. There are water-efficient spray valves offered that supply from 1.6-2.65 gpm at 80psi. These types of sprayers are designed to meet the demands of food service operations.

Ice Making Machines

Ice machines have many commercial uses, from restaurants to lodges, and can use significant amounts of water depending on the type of machine and the desired type of ice. Ice machines are composed of the following components: a condensing unit used for cooling, an evaporator surface for ice formation, an ice harvester, an ice storage container, and, in some models, a dispenser. The type of condenser an ice machine uses will have the largest effect on water use. Two types of condensers are available: air-cooled and water-cooled. Water-cooled machines use 10 times as much water as air-cooled machines and water rarely is recirculated.

In comparing water- and air-cooled compressors, the compressor horsepower at design conditions is invariably higher with air-cooled machining. However, operating costs frequently compare favorably during a full year. The desired quality and visual clarity of ice also will influence water consumption. Ice quality, machine cleaning, and water efficiency all need to be balanced for optimum operation.

Garbage Disposals

Studies show that garbage disposals can waste a significant amount of water. It is recommended that their use be minimized or eliminated from kitchen operations. Many facilities use strainers or traps that employ a mesh screen to collect food waste for proper waste treatment. Another option is to install strainers in sinks, leaving the food matter in the sink for disposal in trash receptacles or composting units.

Quality of the Management

The quality of the management of the foodservice operation will be the most important element in achieving success. Following are typical questions to be addressed by the owners:

— Who will operate the foodservice facility?

— What kind of food experience and educational background must this person have?

— Who will assist this person in covering the long hours that are usually required to operate a foodservice facility?

— What level of pay will this person receive?

— Will this person be rewarded in some way for excellent sales and profit results?

— How will the owners set operational policies and communicate these to the management staff?

The answers to these questions will determine the organizational structure and the kind of management team that will be used to operate the food facility. The successful restaurant often is owned and operated by one individual whose personality becomes a part of the guests' dining experience. On the other hand, the management of the food and beverage department of a hotel may be under the control of more than one person and usually is part of a more complex organizational team.

In this case, the policies and procedures of the food facility should be described in an operations manual to ensure consistent implementation of management policy. From the point of view of the investor or the institutional administration, the management of a food facility must follow traditional management principles of good communication, strong controls, and sound personnel relations regardless of the number of people operating the facility.

The operational philosophy and specific management guidelines to be used in foodservice operations must be carefully considered by the investors in a foodservice facility. Failure to develop management guidelines will very likely lead to the financial failure of the operation.

Method of Execution

The last step in concept development involves operational matters. Although the opening date might seem to be in the distant future to the person planning a food facility, decisions about operating methods must be made during the concept development phase on matters such as production methods, control systems, and personnel.

Production methods

Will convenience foods or traditional "from scratch" cookery be used? This decision will have a great influence on the size of refrigerated and dry storage areas and on the size of the kitchen. Production methods will also determine the number of employees in the kitchen and the skill level of these employees.

Control systems

Food and beverage controls involve many different parts of the facility, and planning for these controls is strongly needed. The following areas of control should be carefully considered:

- Cash control
- Sales analysis
- Guest check control
- Food production forecasting
- Storeroom and refrigeration control
- Back door security
- Labor control
- Purchasing and receiving control

— Quality control

— Portion control

The development of financial feasibility studies cannot begin until the amount of labor required is known. The employee schedules, hours of operation, staffing patterns, staff benefits, skill levels, and level of supervision of employees must all be determined before serious development of the food facility begins. As part of its concept development, the fast-food industry based its low labor costs on the use of hourly unskilled labor, scheduled to work short periods of time. When the food operation is busy, part-time employees are scheduled to work.

The traditional eight-hour day is seldom used in the fast-food industry, except for supervisors and managers. The use of part-time employees in fast-food restaurants has also significantly reduced the cost of benefits. The use of part-time employees was an important part of concept development in the fast-food industry.

Many terms are commonly used in the hospitality industry to describe the process of determining whether or not a food facility is likely to return a profit to its owners. In the case of the financial fea-sibility or ROI (return on investment) analysis, the emphasis is on financial matters such as capital needs, operating funds, cash flow, and return on investment. However, even financial feasibility reports have as their primary focus the determination of whether or not a facility under good management can give investors or owners a return on their investment.

For purposes of explaining the feasibility studies and of guiding the owner, manager, or student into a commonsense approach to these studies, they are classified here into two general categories: those that deal with market feasibility and those that attempt to determine financial feasibility. The two forms of feasibility study can be understood in relation to the financial statements for the operation.

- — The market feasibility study focuses on the income statement and is conducted to determine whether revenues are sufficient to generate a profit.
- — The financial feasibility study focuses on the balance sheet and is conducted to determine whether retained earnings (derived from net income) will be sufficient to satisfy the owners' expectations for a return on their investment.

The primary question addressed in the market feasibility study is: What level of sales revenues can the operation be expected to generate? The answer to this question really cannot be known until the operation has opened; however, building a new restaurant only to find that the sales are insufficient to generate a profit is an expensive lesson. The market feasibility study attempts to project the sales level for the operation before the investors have committed their funds to purchase property, construct a building, and hire a team of employees.

The sales revenue for a foodservice facility is a function of two factors over an appropriate period of time: the number of customers and the price they paid.

$$\text{Sales} = \text{Price} \times \text{Quantity}$$

Market feasibility studies thus have to formulate sales estimates from two separate projections: How many customers will there be? How much will each customer spend? These two estimates are interrelated through the simple economic principle that demand (quantity sold) is more or less a function of price.

Market feasibility studies can be conducted either to test the feasibility of an established foodservice concept or to develop new foodservice concepts that would be appropriate for a given market. Chain restaurant organizations interested in expansion usually want to determine whether, or where, in a given market area their concept would enjoy the greatest opportunity for success.

Independent restaurateurs, as well as chain restaurant organizations, who are interested in developing a new restaurant use the market feasibility study to develop and refine the concept. Because the market feasibility process is complex and time-consuming, it is often conducted by specialized consultants. Independent restaurateurs may find that the cost of engaging a market feasibility consultant is prohibitive. However, it is possible-and certainly advisable-for entrepreneurs to conduct an abbreviated market feasibility study.

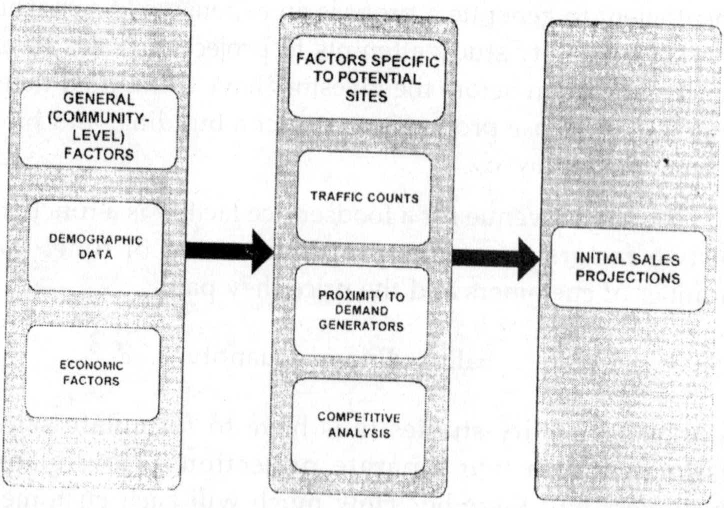

Figure 3.The market feasibility process

Market feasibility studies generally follow the process presented-in simplified and shortened form-in Figure 3. Demographic data and economic factors for the community are analyzed to determine the potential market for the restaurant. Traffic counts and proximity to demand generators are used to assess the viability of possible sites for the restaurant. A competitive analysis is performed to determine whether the market can sustain another restaurant at each potential site. Based on these analyses, sales projections are formulated.

Demographic data include information about the population near the proposed location of the restaurant, including age, income, gender, occupation, number of children at home, home ownership, the use of automobiles, and similar information. These data about individuals are relevant because target market segments for restaurants are often described in terms of the same factors. Demographics thus are known to predict restaurant behavior.

For example, the developers of a casual dinner house may believe that their concept will attract young, single professionals between the ages of twenty-six and thirty-four who have incomes in the $35,000-$50,000 range and who pay monthly rents between $1,000 and $1,600. Obviously, the dinner house should be located where there is a high concentration of individuals who fit the profile of the target market. Gathering demographic data enables the developers to detect the presence of the proposed restaurant's target market segment.

The most comprehensive demographic data are gathered in the decennial U.S. Census. Until recently, using census data involved either extensive library research or access to a mainframe computer. Now, however, detailed census data are available to the public on CD-ROM at a reasonable cost. Also, in the interest of promoting economic growth, many local municipalities have developed extensive databases combining demographic data with information about businesses, organized on detailed maps of the area. This kind of database, called a GIS (geographic information system), gives restaurant developers immediate access to information about the market and the competition.

GIS software and databases also are increasingly available for desktop computers and so bring the resources of high-priced market consultants to the fingertips of entrepreneurs. The prevailing economic climate in a community has a significant impact on the market feasibility of a foodservice operation. The health of the restaurant industry in a local area is closely related to the disposable income of its residents. Generally, when disposable income rises in boom times, restaurants prosper.

In bust times, disposable income falls and restaurants suffer. However, the effects of economic prosperity and depression affect various restaurant concepts differently. Concepts that offer a high degree of perceived value for the price will suffer less than restaurants with high prices. Also, restaurants that draw customers from a particular industry or from a few large, nearby firms may be protected from broader economic fluctuations if the industry or the large firms prosper during down times.

Economic projections for a local area often are available from the chamber of commerce or the local economic development council. New housing developments are an important indicator of economic growth, especially when they are located on the fringes of existing communities. New restaurants often follow new housing developments. County planning commissions usually are quite willing to share information about planned housing developments, new roads, and zoning issues.

Restaurants are usually developed along major thoroughfares. Determining market feasibility requires an estimate of the number of cars that pass by each potential location, which is used in determining which site is optimal. Traffic counts can usually be obtained free of charge from the local chamber of commerce, highway department, mayor's office, tourism agency, or other municipal offices.

Some fast-food chains have developed very exact specifications for locating a good site for the foodservice facilities. For instance, one of the guidelines for placement of a Kentucky Fried Chicken (KFC) outlet is that it be located on the "going-home side of the street," for obvious reasons. Other chains have minimum community size, minimum traffic count, and minimum average income standards that must be met before consideration will be given to building or franchising on a particular site.

Demand generators

Demand generators are destinations that draw extensive traffic, such as shopping malls, recreation and sports facilities, and public facilities such as museums, zoos, and parks. Restaurants located near demand generators benefit from the traffic they produce as, for example, when shoppers have lunch after visiting the local mall.

For some foodservice concepts, proximity to other restaurants enhances rather than hurts market feasibility. Fast-food concepts, for example, often locate in clusters along interstate highway interchanges. Similarly, cities and suburbs often have a "restaurant row" in commercial areas.

A competitive analysis is crucial to the market feasibility study because the local market potential for a given concept must be shared among all of the competitors. If demographic research identifies an area that has a sales potential of $6 million to $8 million for casual dinner houses, it is important to know how many already are in operation. Moreover, when the restaurateur identifies an area that appears to be ripe for development, he or she should assume that the competition will soon arrive. Most chain restaurant organizations have access to GIS market data, and many of them use those data extensively to identify prime development opportunities.

An independent restaurant entrepreneur who is conducting a market feasibility analysis should identify all the similar concepts within the geographic area, compare menus and prices, and count seats. More importantly, he or she should count customers at various times during the week at the restaurants that would be the closest competition. If patrons are lined up outside the doors to get a seat on Monday or Tuesday night, that is good news. However, if there is no waiting at the competition on Friday or Saturday night, the independent restaurateur should look elsewhere. It is also important to take seasonal factors into account. Counting cars and customers at the competition during the summer months will bias estimates upward, just as counts taken during the winter when two feet (610 millimeters) of snow are on the ground may bias estimates downward.

Sales projections are informed by the information gathered about demographics, economic factors, traffic patterns, demand generators, and competitive analysis. Recall that sales projections are composed of estimates about quantity (number of customers) and price. Demographic data indicate the relative size of the local population and thus are useful in projecting the number of customers (quantity). Income information may also be found in demographic data and may thus assist in estimating the price range that people are willing to accept.

Economic factors are especially important in projecting price. Entrepreneurs often make the mistake of basing their sales estimates on data gathered during boom times and thus find themselves suffering during bust times. Traffic pattern data are crucial in estimating customer counts, as is the presence of demand generators. Competitive analysis helps the entrepreneur determine his or her share of the customer market and predict price points against the competition.

The weakness in many market feasibility studies can be found within the sales projection section. This part of the feasibility report is often the first place that a banker will look to determine the accuracy of the financial forecast. Bankers always appreciate conservative sales projections that reflect the restaurateur's planning for sales fluctuations during difficult periods. Restaurant entrepreneurs also often overestimate the dining patterns and price sensitivities of the local market. Sometimes this is the result of wishful thinking, but other times it is the result of insufficient planning and preparation. A valuable way for the entrepreneur to check his or her assumptions about the market is to develop a questionnaire and distribute it to those who reside or work in the area.

The lending institution, investor, owner, and manager will all want to know the financial projections for the planned new or renovated food facility. Each of these persons will, of course, have a different set of reasons for seeking the projections, and each will want data from the projections presented in a different manner. For instance, the banker will be looking in part for the ratio of invested capital to borrowed capital. The banker may also want to know the amount of operating cash and the cash flow from sales that will be involved in the operation.

The manager needs to know what his or her budget is and what the expectation of the owner is concerning profit and loss. The manager and the banker probably will not be using the same financial reports and projections, but they certainly will be getting their information from the same original source, which will probably be the financial feasibility study.

Usually in the financial feasibility study two basic documents-the projected balance sheet and the pro forma profit-and-loss statement-are prepared, along with other supporting reports and schedules. A good outline of the kind of information that must be projected can be made by examining the line items on each of these documents.

A simple comparative balance sheet, illustrates the kind of data that must be determined. This balance sheet is a simplification of the projected comparative balance sheet that should be developed under the guidance of the firm's accountant. The balance sheet illustrates a number of projections that must be made by the person or firm preparing the financial feasibility study. On the asset side of the balance sheet:

— The amount of cash needed as operating funds

— The amount of cash tied up in food inventory

— The investment in land and building

— The cash needed for a down payment on land and building

— The cost of furniture, fixtures, equipment, and utensils

— The cost of parking lots, driveways, lighting, and other improvements to the property.

PREPEARING PRO-FORMA PROFIT-AND LOSS STATEMENT

The pro forma profit-and-loss (P&L) statement should be prepared by the owner, manager, or other persons who will be involved in the management of the food facility. This statement projects the income and expense for a particular period of time. For the financial feasibility study, a three-to-five-year projection would be considered sufficient. The format for the P&L should follow the Uniform System of Accounts developed for hotels and restaurants for income and expense categories that fit the needs of the food operation.

Several supporting schedules are prepared to supplement the P&L statement. Because food and labor costs combined typically run between 60 and 80 percent of sales revenue, schedules providing detailed information on how the cost of food sales and the cost of personnel and related expenses were calculated are often provided.

A schedule detailing how the amount shown on the cost-of-sales line of the P&L statement was calculated is often prepared. Because the cost of sales for the menu equals the selling price minus the cost of the ingredients used in preparation, two closely related steps are involved in preparing the schedule: determining the portion cost for each menu item and estimating the price for each menu item.

The portion cost for each menu item is determined by examining the recipe and costs for each ingredient. The form provides the following information:

— A list of all food ingredients

— The portion size of each ingredient

— The cost of each ingredient

— The total portion cost

If the menu price includes the meat, vegetable, dessert, and beverage, then the above example would necessarily include a complete list of all foods that are a part of this meal. A small amount ($.05) might be added to cover the cost of seasonings and other condiments.

The two traditional methods for determining the selling price for menu items are (a) to divide the portion cost by a set percentage (the desired food cost percentage for the operation), and (b) to add a set dollar amount to the cost. Using the first pricing approach, a manager who seeks to have a 32 percent food cost percentage would divide the food cost of a menu item by the desired percentage.

A third approach to setting prices involves looking not at each item but at the menu and menu mix (the quantity sold of each menu item) as a whole. The goal of this approach is to set prices so that the contribution margin (the amount of revenue remaining when the cost of sales has been subtracted from revenue) is sufficient to pay all expected fixed expenses and satisfy the owner's expectations for a returr ɔn investment. A spreadsheet can be used to estimate the overall cost of sales by building from the cost of each menu item. It shows columns for the projected price, the portion cost, the contribution margin (price minus cost), the menu item cost percentage (cost divided by price), the projected quantity sold (the menu mix), the total sales (price multiplied by quantity), the total cost (portion cost multiplied by quantity), the total cost (cost multiplied by quantity), and the total contribution (contribution multiplied by quantity) for each menu item.

The advantage of the spreadsheet approach over traditional strategies to pricing, such as simply marking up the cost by a given percentage or dollar amount, is that prices can be set to generate the maximum contribution margin. In foodservice, profits come not from minimizing the food cost percentage but from maximizing the contribution margin. However, for the purposes of preparing the pro forma profit-and-loss statement, the overall food cost percentage derived from the spread-sheet can be used to estimate the cost of sales.

Finally, it is essential to check the competition in setting prices for each menu item, because an operation that is not competitively priced will suffer. Once the menu pricing and preferred menu mix have been established, the calculation of the cost of food sales is simple: The projected sales revenue is multiplied by the overall food cost factor, and the result is shown on the pro forma P&L statement.

COST CONTROLS

Managing expenses is among the most important things a manager does. The most central elements of effective expense management are proactive rather than reactive.

The first step in expense management is budgeting, and zero-based budgeting is best. Sure, one can look at many historical expenses, anticipate what they are likely to be in the future and put that in the budget. While that gets the budget done, it does not actually help manage the expense. One needs to look at the historical expense, analyze what its components are, decide how it can be improved and finally, implement those changes.

The cost of guest room cleaning supplies and laundry supplies do not consist solely of the purchase price. The cost actually includes theft, loss, spillage, improper dilution and dispensing, and improper use. Improper use of laundry supplies might include running less than full loads in a washer or having it set for the wrong fabric. In the case of room cleaning supplies, it might include overuse of chemicals or not truly wearing out a sponge before it is discarded.

As part of the budgeting process, each component of an expense needs to be examined with an eye on how it can be reduced. In many cases, individual steps can be changed, while in other cases, it may be a common thread through an entire department. These may be attitudinal, process, training or physical layout issues. In most cases, individual items, once they are identified, are easily correctable.

Process and training issues are sometimes more difficult and time consuming to identify and address. A good example of a process issue may be the number of minutes per occupied room it may take Room Attendants to clean rooms.

First, one needs to insure that they are measuring accurately and that the goal is achievable. The next step is to examine the process by which Room Attendants start their day, take breaks and finish their day along with how cleaning supplies and linen are stocked. In a 150 room hotel with 60% occupancy with an average housekeeping wage of $5.00 per hour plus 25% for mandatory and discretionary benefits a minute of Room Attendant time per occupied room is worth $3,422 per year. Clearly saving five or ten minutes can add up to a lot of money, so why not examine every step a Room Attendant makes? Why not have the linen folded in the laundry so it fits on the carts without refolding? Why not have the supplies delivered directly to the carts while the Room Attendants are at lunch and again at the end of the day?

One person or a team can stock all the carts identically much more quickly than a group of individuals doing it their own way at their own way at their own pace, including returning for forgotten items after standing around chatting for a minute or two. In many cases, supplies are being delivered to linen closets and shelved. Subsequently, the items have to be moved from the shelf to the cart.

When the Room Attendant finally gets to a room, every step should be carefully scripted and wasted motion eliminated. Why not dust the headboard, art work, bedside tables and lights while the bed spread is being adjusted around the pillows? Simply keep a dust rag in their pocket. Every step and motion should be examined with input from the Housekeeper and several of the hotel's best Room Attendants.

As the budget is developed, various plans evolve for every department from Front Office to Engineering. If part of the budget assumptions are that the Average Daily Rate (ADR) is going to be in-creased by upselling and suggestive selling, then a training plan has to be created for the employees who will be making the sales effort. If HVAC maintenance costs can be reduced by doing more of the work on this equipment by the hotel staff rather than contractors, then somebody either needs to be trained or additional staff hired and trained.

The important thing is that the budget must be detailed in its assumptions and in its implementation. If certain staffing assumptions are used for a restaurant, then the person doing the staff scheduling for that restaurant must be verified that those assumptions are being applied each week when the restaurant's schedule is prepared.

Steps to Food Cost Control

1. *Ordering*: The first step is to order right. Having detailed recipes, designing purchasing specifications, doing comparative shopping based on those specifications, and comparing quality, price and service, etc. Don't order too early in order to avoid spoilage, wasted storage space and lost interest on your money. Don't order too late, so premium costs and delivery charges accrue.
2. *Receiving*: The fundamentals are obvious: count; weigh; inspect for condition and quality; verify against the purchase order; keep the receiving area clean and uncluttered; limit access to the receiving area; train the person receiving and make him or her responsible. Get credit memos from the delivery driver.
3. *Storing*: Is the method and place of storage for the various items appropriate for the item? Is it secure from pilferage? Are the shelves strong enough for the product, allow air circulation and easy to clean? Are all items stored at a temperature appropriate for that product? Are items dated and priced?
4. *Issuing*: What is issuing based on? Who has access and or authority to issue or take things from the secured store rooms and walk-ins? Are issues being made in appropriate quantities and at appropriate times? Is there a relationship to volume or reasonable par stocks? Are issues being accounted for? Is a perpetual inventory or sign out sheet designed specifically for your operation or a particular store room in use?

5. *Preperation*: Phrases related to preperation include: trim properly; use trimmings for stock pots and other recipes. Proper tools, sharp knives, clean and neat working area, enforcing a policy of following recipes, and having photos of finished products available and used regularly are also critical.

6. *Coocking*: Proper temperatures, proper cooking times, following recipes carefully, using photographs of finished products, correct size, material, and type of utensils and cookware, clean work area.

7. *Serving*: Serving is not only about portion control, it is also about decisions made regarding portion size and presentation. With a buffet, it is obvious. Proper serving utensils, proper holding/serving equipment, right presentation order, plate sizes, etc. In a bar its easy, too. Jiggers or other measuring and control devices and very strict discipline. Dining room service should be easy to control using good kitchen supervisors, trained cooks, photographs for both cooks and servers, etc. Watch what comes back from bused tables to see if portions are proper. Marketing decisions may drive large portions but if the patrons are not eating it or taking it home, the portion size or the recipe should be reconsidered.

8. *Training*: Work hard on your cost controls and be consistent about them. One element of controlling food cost covers all seven categories: thorough training. Give your staff the ability and knowledge and confidence to do their jobs properly and to your specifications. Inconsistency and failure to enforce procedures will drive costs skyward. Failure here is like throwing money away.

4

Food Processing

Designing a Food Processing Unit

There are some of the design errors, commonly visible in many of the food factories, which are facing quality management problems. It is important to note that it is very difficult to ensure food safety and quality in badly designed food factories. It is also observed that, the maintenance and operation cost of badly designed food factories is very high. This means, such companies are losing on both fronts i.e. their production costs goes up and the manufactured products are also of inferior quality. This all happens when the architects and the consultants involved in designing food factories gives more importance to external beauty of the building and other comforts for managers than the functional need of the food factories which are essential features of good manufacturing practices. While designing a food factory or processing unit the two basic features should be given top most priority:

— Cleanability

— Durability

In order to ensure cleanliness, without compromising on safety of workers and food safety in the factory, following points, which are vital, should be considered.

Floors, Walls, and Ceilings

The floors, floor coverings, walls, wall coverings, and ceilings in food processing factories can be source of contamination therefore they should be designed, constructed, and installed in such a manner that they are smooth and easily cleanable. There are various construction materials available now-a-days but selection criteria should consider the requirements of the process like hot water, acid, alkali, cleaning materials, spillage, etc. At the same time precautions should be taken to ensure anti-slip floor coverings may be used for safety reasons in work areas.

Utility Lines

Common utilities for any food factories are like tap water, hot water, compressed air, steam, electricity, etc. Utility service lines and other pipes may not be unnecessarily exposed because these can be ideal place for accumulation of dirt and dust and breeding ground for contamination. At the same time, exposed utility service lines and pipes should be installed in such a way so that they do not obstruct or prevent cleaning of the floors, walls, or ceilings or movement of goods and people when required. Exposed horizontal utility service lines and pipes should not be installed on the floor to avoid smooth movement of goods and people when required.

Floor and Wall Junctures

Floor and Wall Junctures are critical points. In food establishments in which cleaning methods other than water flushing are used for cleaning floors, the floor and wall junctures should be covered and closed to no larger than 1 mm. The floors in food establishments in which water flush cleaning methods are used should be provided with drains and be graded to drain, and the floor and wall junctures should be covered and properly sealed.

Floor Carpeting and Attachments

All floor coverings such as carpeting or similar material may not be installed as a floor covering in food preparation areas where the floor is subject to moisture, flushing, or spray cleaning methods like walk-in cold-storage, ware-washing areas, toilet room areas, refuse storage rooms, or other areas

If carpeting is installed as a floor covering in areas other than those specified above, it should be:

— Securely attached to the floor, by using a stretch and tack method, or by another method; and

— Installed tightly against the wall under the covering or installed away from the wall with a space between the carpet and the wall and with the edges of the carpet secured by metal stripping or some other means.

— Temporary coverings like mats should be designed to be removable and easily cleanable. At the same time, Wall and ceiling covering materials should be attached so that they are easily cleanable.

— Areas used for dry storage only, concrete, porous blocks, or bricks used for indoor wall construction should be finished and sealed to provide a smooth, non-absorbent, easily cleanable surface.

— Not only Walls and Ceilings but also attachments to walls and ceilings such as light fixtures, mechanical room ventilation system components, vent covers, wall mounted fans, decorative items, and other attachments should be easily cleanable.

Functionality of Factory Design is very important, otherwise the cost of rectification of quality problems and maintenance of factory will be very expensive.

Light Bulbs with Protective Shielding

Light bulbs should be shielded, coated, or otherwise shatter-resistant in areas where there is exposed food; clean equipment, utensils, and linens; or unwrapped single-service and single-use articles. An infrared or other heat lamp should be protected against breakage by a shield surrounding and extending beyond the bulb so that only the face of the bulb is exposed.

Heating, Ventilating, Air Conditioning System Vents and Ducts

Heating, ventilating, and air conditioning systems should be designed and installed in such a manner that make-up air intake and exhaust vents do not cause contamination of food, food-contact surfaces, equipment, or utensils. Proper air filters and air cleaning system should be followed and properly maintained. Selection of air filters will depend upon the flow rates and quality of air required.

Design and Installation of Insect Control Devices

Insect control devices that are used to electrocute or stun flying insects should be designed to retain the insect within the device. Insect control devices should be installed so that the devices are not located over a food preparation area; and dead insects and insect fragments are prevented from being impelled onto or falling on exposed food; clean equipment, utensils, and linens; and unwrapped single-service and single-use articles. At the same time devices are installed in such a manner that it should not become obstruction to the smooth movement of man and material and should not cause any harm to the employees due to prolonged exposure.

Toilet Rooms

The toilet rooms located in the premises should be completely enclosed and provided with a tight-fitting and self-closing door. This requirement does not apply to the toilet room that is located outside the food establishments and does not open directly into the food establishment areas for e.g. toilet room that is provided by the management in the administrative area away from the food production area.

Outer Openings like windows and doors

Outer openings, like windows and doors of a food establishment should be protected against the entry of insects and rodents by filling or closing holes and other gaps and sloops along floors, walls and ceilings; also by closed, tight-fitting windows; and Solid self-closing and tight-fitting doors.

If the windows or doors of a food establishment, or of a larger structure within which a food establishment is located, are kept open for ventilation or other purposes it should be protected against the entry of insects and rodents. Combinations of insect resistant screen; properly designed and installed air curtains; or other effective means can achieve the purpose.

Exterior Walls and Roofs and Gardens

Perimeter walls and roofs of a food establishment should effectively protect the establishment from the weather and the entry of insects, rodents, and other animals. Very often the gardens and trees around the food factories act as a breeding ground for insects and rodents and is an ideal place for birds nesting.

Outdoor Walking and Driving Surfaces

Exterior walking and driving surfaces should be graded to drain to avoid water logging. Exterior walking and driving surfaces should be made of easily cleanable material and should not act as a source of contamination.

Outdoor Refuse Areas

Outdoor refuse areas should be constructed in accordance with provisions of law and should be curbed and graded to drain, to collect and to dispose of liquid waste that results from the refuse.

Change Rooms

Change rooms provided for lodging and rest of workers should be separated from rooms and areas used for food establishment operations by complete partitioning and solid self-closing doors.

All washrooms, lunchrooms and change rooms should be separate from the food processing areas and should be properly ventilated and maintained. Washrooms should be equipped with a sufficient number of properly installed sinks and plumbed with hot and cold potable water.

Processing areas and areas where employees are in direct contact with microbiologically sensitive product should contain conveniently located hand-washing stations controlled by foot, knee or a timer with sensors.

Clear signs should be posted in these areas, in appropriate languages, requiring employees to wash their hands.

Outdoor food handling areas

Storage area, despatch and other food handling areas should be provided with proper overhead protection. Areas used only for the loading of water or the discharge of sewage and other liquid waste, through the use of a closed system of hoses, need not be provided with overhead protection.

Food Processing Equipment and Machinery in GMPs

Properly designed food factories can only provide protective covering but the role of properly designed machines is as vital as the quality of raw material. Food machines are contact surfaces in food establishment, any negligence while selecting food machines can be as fatal as selecting an inferior quality of raw material for processing. While selecting and designing any food processing or handling equipment we must consider the following attributes of the system:

Durability and Strength

Equipment and utensils shall be designed and constructed to be durable and to retain their characteristic qualities under normal use conditions. This is essential because food factories most of the time runs round the year and in various climatic conditions. At the same time food as well as workers safety should be the integral part of the design. Food temperature measuring devices may not have sensors or stems constructed of glass, except that thermometers with glass sensors or stems that are encased in a shatterproof coating.

Cleanability

Food-Contact Surfaces: In order to ensure cleanability, multiuse food-contact surfaces shall be

— Smooth;

— Free of breaks, open seams, cracks, chips, pits, and similar imperfections;

— Free of sharp internal angles, corners, and crevices;

— Finished to have smooth welds and joints; and

— Accessible for cleaning and inspection by one of the following methods:

1. Without being disassembled,
2. By disassembling without the use of tools, or
3. By easy disassembling with the use of handheld tools commonly available to maintenance and cleaning personnel such as screwdrivers, pliers, open-end wrenches, etc.

Accuracy

The food processing equipment must ensure accuracy for processing parameters. Accuracy is vital to ensure proper processing of foods. Under-processing may lead to serious food safety hazard and over-processing leads to deterioration of food quality and nutrients, high cost of production due to over spending of energy and uncomfortable working conditions. In extreme cases it can be a serious safety hazard.

Accuracy is required for:

— Temperature Measuring Devices

— Pressure Measuring Devices

Temperature Measuring Devices: In a mechanically refrigerated or hot food storage unit, the sensor of a temperature measuring device shall be located to measure the air temperature in the warmest part of a mechanically refrigerated unit and in the coolest part of a hot food storage unit.

Temperature measuring devices shall be designed to be easily readable. Food temperature measuring devices and water temperature measuring devices on ware-washing machines shall have a numerical scale, printed record, or digital readout in increments no greater than 1°C or 2°F in the intended range of use.

Food temperature measuring devices that are scaled only in Celsius or dually scaled in Celsius and Fahrenheit shall be accurate to 1°C in the intended range of use. Food temperature measuring devices that are scaled only in Fahrenheit shall be accurate to 2°F in the intended range of use.

Ambient air and water temperature measuring devices that are scaled in Celsius or dually scaled in Celsius and Fahrenheit shall be designed to be easily readable and accurate to 1.5°C in the intended range of use. Ambient air and water temperature measuring devices that are scaled only in Fahrenheit shall be accurate to 3°F in the intended range of use.

Pressure measuring devices that display the pressures in the water supply line for the fresh hot water sanitising rinse shall have increments of 7 kilopascals or smaller and shall be accurate to 14 kilopascals in the 100-170 kilopascals (15-25 pounds per square inch) range.

Functionality

In order to maintain the good working condition inside food factory and proper maintenance of the equipment, the functionality of the machines must be properly considered.

Ventilation Hood Systems, Drip Prevention

Exhaust ventilation hood systems in food preparation and warewashing areas including components such as hoods, fans, guards, and ducting shall be designed to prevent grease or condensation from draining or dripping onto food, equipment, utensils, linens, and single-service and single-use articles.

Equipment Openings, Closures and Deflectors

A cover or lid for equipment shall overlap the opening and be sloped to drain.

— An opening located within the top of a unit of equipment that is designed for use with a cover or lid shall be flanged upward at least 5 millimetres.

— If a watertight joint is not provided:

— The piping, temperature measuring devices, rotary shafts, and other parts extending through the openings shall be equipped with an apron designed to deflect condensation, drips, and dust from openings into the food; and

— The opening shall be flanged.

Dispensing Equipment, Protection of Equipment and Food

In equipment that dispenses or vends liquid food or ice in unpackaged form:

— The delivery tube, chute, orifice, and splash surfaces directly above the container receiving the food shall be designed in a manner, such as with barriers, baffles, or drip aprons, so that drips from condensation and splash are diverted from the opening of the container receiving the food;

— The delivery tube, chute, and orifice shall be protected from manual contact such as by being recessed;

— The delivery tube or chute and orifice of equipment used to vend liquid food or ice in unpackaged form to self-service consumers shall be designed so that the delivery tube or chute and orifice are protected from dust, insects, rodents, and other contamination by a self-closing door if the equipment is:

— Located in an outside area that does not otherwise afford the protection of an enclosure against the rain, windblown debris, insects, rodents, and other contaminants that are present in the environment, or

— Available for self-service during hours when it is not under the full-time supervision of a food employee; and

— The dispensing equipment actuating lever or mechanism and filling device of consumer self-service beverage dispensing equipment shall be designed to prevent contact with the lip-contact surface of glasses or cups that are refilled.

Vending Machine, Vending Stage Closure

The dispensing compartment of a vending machine including a machine that is designed to vend prepackaged snack food that is not potentially hazardous such as chips, party mixes, and pretzels shall be equipped with a self-closing door or cover if the machine is:

— Located in an outside area that does not otherwise afford the protection of an enclosure against the rain, windblown debris, insects, rodents, and other contaminants that are present in the environment; or

— Available for self-service during hours when it is not under the full-time supervision of a food employee.

Bearings and Gear Boxes, Leakproof

Equipment containing bearings and gears that require lubricants shall be designed and constructed so that the lubricant can not leak, drip, or be forced into food or onto food-contact surfaces. Selection of lubricant is equally crucial.

PEST CONTROL IN FOOD PROCESSING

The lack of proper sanitation procedures can cost plant operators a lot of money. Often this loss is not obvious to management. It shows up in terms of customers going elsewhere, poor employee morale, unreported spoilage problems or poor food quality in restaurants (resulting in lack of repeat business). More obvious to management are direct complaints and government intervention ranging from the local county sanitarian to FDA to USDA inspectors. Lack of proper sanitation can cause increased returns of products, shorter shelf life, less profit and can invite the threat of possible operation shutdown.

The condition of the outside of your plant is important in making a good first impression. If the outside area is unkempt, it is likely that the water supply, waste disposal, and sewage disposal systems suffer also. Regulations govern the water supply in plants that use well water. Test the water periodically to determine potability. Make sure that no back siphonage can occur throughout the plant. Generally, sewage disposal and liquid waste disposal are also governed by regulations. Plants that use lagoon systems must closely monitor the effluent to make sure the lagoon is not becoming overloaded. It is imperative that a member of the quality control team keep records of the Biological Oxygen Demand (BOD) as well as suspended solids and other pertinent information dealing with the effluent.

The importance of dry waste disposal is often overlooked in food processing plants as well as fast food outlets, hospitals, school cafeterias, etc. Unfortunately, this is sometimes looked on as a necessary evil and very little time is allocated to the cleaning of dry waste disposal units. Very small amounts of accumulated food debris left in the bottom of a trash container can be the food source and breeding area for literally millions of flies and other pests, not to mention multitudes of microorganisms.

Use a scraper or hoe to loosen the caked material at the bottom of the trash container, then wash and spray it. This can disrupt the cycle and eliminate this particular source of insect infestation. Remember, research has shown that a single housefly is capable of carrying six and a half million bacteria, many of which may be pathogenic.

Bacteria, like other forms of life, are confronted with the critical struggle for existence. They must have food, moisture and ideal temperature for growth. Bacteria have no way of migrating from one area to another or from one person to another. This means they must be conveyed by some sort of "carrier." If the type of conveyance is interrupted, the continuous scattering of bacteria can be controlled. This can be accomplished by utilizing a good cleaning program that includes an improved method of washing, rinsing, and sanitizing of all utensils and equipment after use. Write out the sanitation program of a plant in specific terms so that any new employee coming on the job can follow the instructions and know exactly what to do.

Cleaning is the removal of dirt or debris by physical and/or chemical means.

Sanitizing is the process used to rid or reduce the number of microbes (microorganisms) on the surface. Sanitizing cannot be accomplished until surfaces are clean. Sanitizing cannot be effective without a good pest control program.

Pest Control is the reduction or eradication of pests (macroorganisms). These include flies, cockroaches, mice and rats, as well as weevils and other insects that can infest food products. Pest control cannot be effectively accomplished unless and until proper clearing has occurred.

If no pests are present, cleaning followed by sanitizing is sufficient. If, however, pests are present, they must be controlled before the sanitizing step. This is because the pests will recontaminate any surface that may have been sanitized.

There are five steps that should take place when cleaning an area:

Remove debris

Never use a hose when a squeegee, broom or shovel can be used. In a processing plant, use a shovel to move such items as eggshells, meat scraps, chicken parts or vegetables. Place these in containers or troughs, or on conveyors that will remove the debris from the plant. Food wastes may be removed via truck to a rendering plant, landfill, or dryer.

In a restaurant or institution (such as hospitals, nursing homes, jails or schools), use a long handled dustpan to pick up solid items, paper and other trash. Never dry sweep in areas where food is on display or customers are eating. A damp mop may be used to contain spilled liquids. Place food residues in well marked, plastic lined garbage containers. Tie plastic bags shut prior to placing them in a Dumpster for removal. In the kitchen, scrape utensils of any excess food particles or burned on foodstuffs.

In the home, put food remains from plates, cutting boards and counter tops in the disposal or wrap them and put them in a garbage can or Dumpster.

Rinse

Most food processing plants are required to have a floor drain every 400 square feet. Hose down (with water) any remaining small particles of fish, meat, poultry, vegetables, milk or egg liquids. This prepares the surfaces for the next step. Take care to avoid spraying water directly on motors and other electrical equipment. If metal bars are used to raise belts, don't run the equipment with bars in place. This will damage the belts and possibly the equipment. Disassemble equipment, such as band saws, pipes, stuffers, etc.

A thorough rinse with cold or tepid water will make the next step more effective. Remember, some proteins coagulate at 140°F to 145°F. Never use excessively hot water or steam; this would bake the protein onto equipment much as an egg sticks to an ungreased frying pan.

Cleaning is not finished until the drains are cleaned. However, use care when using water in food warehouses. Do not allow moisture to come in contact with dry goods stored in the building. Clean coolers containing wet products such as meat, fish, poultry, milk, vegetables, etc., on a regular basis. Make sure someone is responsible for cleaning and sanitizing often overlooked areas, such as floor drains.

Depending on the construction, the kitchen of a restaurant or institution may be treated similarly to a processing plant. If floor drains are scarce, it may be necessary to use the old-fashioned mop and bucket. Soak utensils and other items difficult to clean, such as grinders, mixer parts, beaters, whisks, etc., in 120°F water to begin loosening the debris. This is generally referred to as presoaking.

In the home, everyone knows the value of presoaking hard to clean pots and pans. Your dishwasher may have a presoak cycle built in. Although a part of the next step, a little detergent added here sometimes helps to loosen stubborn baked on food particles.

Detergent Application

Some food plants and warehouses are equipped with high-pressure sprayers through which detergent is metered. The loosening action of the detergent, together with the high water pressure, removes the residue from the equipment surfaces. Another method of applying detergent is by foaming it on the equipment and allowing it to work for a few minutes prior to the next step of rinsing. Certain pieces of equipment need to be cleaned manually using brushes, steel pads, etc.

In most states, restaurants and institutions are required to have a four-compartment sink. The first compartment is used to rinse off large particles of adhering soil. The second compartment is used to apply the detergent in 120° to 140°F water. The third compartment is used to rinse and the fourth to sanitize. Brush or agitate in some manner equipment that has been disassembled to facilitate removal of debris. Detergents are manufactured to do specific jobs. Therefore, make a decision on whether to use low foaming versus high foaming or alkaline versus acid detergent when consulting with the manufacturer's representative.

Rinse

After applying detergent by high-pressure spray, soak tank or foaming, rinse the equipment with clean potable water. It is extremely important that all detergent residue is completely rinsed off since very small amounts of detergent in food can cause stomach and intestinal disorders similar to the symptoms of food poisoning. In a restaurant or institution, the third compartment of the sink is used for rinsing. In the home, dishes are rinsed and placed in a rack to air dry. Water for rinsing should be 180°F.

Sanitize

There are several general classes of sanitizers. These include:

— Halogens—chlorine, iodine, and bromine

— Phenols

— Quaternary Ammonium Compounds

Consider the following items when selecting a sanitizer for your particular operation:

— The length of time the sanitizer will be in contact with the surface to be sanitized. If you are going to soak the equipment, then the rate of sanitizing action is relatively unimportant.

— The temperature at which the sanitizer will be used. For example, in the case of chlorine, as the temperature is increased, chlorine is less effective.

— The amount of organic material (fats, proteins, vegetable materials, etc.) present in or on the equipment to be sanitized. If the equipment to be sanitized contains many particles of organic matter in addition to bacteria, the sanitizer will concentrate on the organic particles and combine with them rather than the much smaller bacteria. On the other hand, if the equipment is relatively clean and if bacteria comprise the majority of the particulate matter on the equipment, then the sanitizer will be more effective.

— The cost of the sanitizer. No matter how efficient a sanitizer may be, its cost may limit its application. Before selecting a sanitizer, review all considerations in order to determine the most economical one to use for a particular job.

— The sanitizer's pH. It is important to know the pH of the solution in which the sanitizer will be expected to act. Again, using chlorine as an example, we find that the lower the pH, the more effective chlorine is as a sanitizing agent.

The bactericidal effectiveness of a chemical sanitizer can be measured by determining its Phenol Coefficient. This value is obtained by comparing the sanitizer's activity with a pure Phenol. A Phenol is a highly toxic agent to all bacteria under carefully standardized conditions. The test is made by separately mixing various concentrations of Phenol and sanitizer with known numbers of bacteria. After a specific time limit, the solutions are compared for total kill.

The highest dilution of the test sanitizing solution that kills all the organisms in ten minutes is divided by the highest dilution of Phenol giving the same results, to give the Phenol Coefficient (P). For example, if the highest dilution d the test solution that gives 100 percent kill in ten minutes is 1-500 and for Phenol, 1-100, the Phenol Coefficient is P = 500 100 = 5. Phenol Coefficients are calculated by the manufacturers of sanitizers in order to determine recommended concentrations for use in solution. Thus, the higher the Phenol Coefficient, the more effective that particular sanitizer is in killing bacteria. With a tremendous number of detergents and sanitizers now being marketed and with some new product being introduced every day, there are innumerable formulations of cleaning compounds from which to choose.

Almost every cleaning job has a detergent designed to handle it. We must become familiar with the proper use of detergents for various jobs. Any cleaning compound used on product contact surfaces or in processing areas should be approved by USDA. The United States Department of Agriculture Consumer and Marketing Service, Consumer Protection Programs, Technical Service Division, publishes a list alphabetized by company of chemical compounds that are approved for use in food operations. Although this list was compiled for food processors manufacturing products under USDA Poultry, Meat, Rabbit, and Egg Products Inspectors Programs, it could be used as a guide for the safe use of detergents and sanitizers in any food related situation.

Dip utensils, equipment parts, etc., in a chemical solution or in 180°F water for 30 seconds to complete the sanitizing process. Sanitize stationary equipment by use of a small pump sprayer in a small plant or by use of a high-pressure sprayer in a larger facility. A small hand held spray type bottle may be used in a restaurant for table sanitizing. Probably the most generally used sanitizer is chlorine. The ability of any sanitizer to inactivate or kill microorganisms is dependent upon the germicidal action of the sanitizer itself (i.e., its selectivity and concentration, the length of time during which the sanitizer is in contact with the surface being sanitized, the number and characteristics of the microflora present, the temperature, the pH and the amount of organic matter and other incompatible materials, such as mineral deposits). The greater the number of microorganisms present, the more difficult it is to effectively remove them. Certain sanitizers are more effective or have a greater germicidal action than others. For instance, chlorine can be purchased in the form of sodium hypochlorite in 5, 11, and 15 percent solutions.

Naturally, less quantity of the 15 percent solution is needed than that of the 5 percent solution. If mineral deposits, milkstone or other incompatible materials are present on the surface, sanitizers cannot penetrate to the bacteria and therefore, the cost of the sanitizers is wasted. You cannot sanitize dirt. When choosing a sanitizer, take care to determine the surface makeup of the equipment that is to be sanitized.

If chlorine is used in high concentrations on stainless steel equipment, pitting of the equipment will eventually occur since chlorine in solution forms an acid. Likewise, the use of iodophores on belts and other pieces of equipment that can absorb sanitizers tend to stain the equipment. Do not use phenols in food processing plants. The odor of a phenol can penetrate food materials, causing undesirable flavors and odors in the food.

They are at times used in restrooms, and it is difficult to determine whether or not the restroom has been cleaned or the phenol compound has simply been spilled in the area masking the odor of a restroom. Quaternary ammonium compounds (QUATS) have a use in food processing plants. However, their use has been limited due to the cost of these compounds.

Examination of this passage of the Act reveals that any food product containing filth may be in violation if it is even held under conditions where food may become contaminated, regardless of whether it is a hazard to health. Regulatory action can be taken if food becomes contaminated, or is prepared, packed or held under conditions where it could become contaminated with insect fragments, rodent hair, bird feathers, feces, etc.

Top management is ultimately responsible for identifying a competent person to develop a pest prevention and control program. Give them the necessary support to carry out the program and ensure that pesticides are used in accordance with label instructions. Persons who apply pesticides in industrial and institutional settings have a responsibility to use the needed pesticide, to apply it correctly (according to label instructions), and to be certain there is no hazard to man or the environment. Guard against the spread of microorganisms and filth by flying and crawling insects, rats, mice, and other vermin.

Pest control is often ignored until pests and their damage are discovered. For example, if rodents or insects are found in a food storage room, temporary measures are taken to eliminate them. The real trouble, however, is not corrected. This situation needs a sustained effort, including: inspecting incoming food for evidence of insects or rodents before storing it, rodent proofing the room, storing the food off the floor, keeping the room clean, and inspecting the room for insect and rodent activity on a regular basis.

The method of treating a single outbreak is a poor concept of sanitation. In the heavily regulated food industry, this could be disastrous since contaminated food can be seized and destroyed and fines levied against the company. Embarrassment, bad publicity and economic loss to an industry or institution can sometimes be worse than regulatory actions. Take every fitting precaution to exclude the pests from all sections of the processing plant.

Eliminate cracks and crevices in food storage and handling areas by proper construction or repairs. A tight, waterproof, smooth surface is easier to clean and keep clean. Properly construct concrete block, poured concrete or brick walls to eliminate cracks and pores that could offer insects shelter or access.

Make all food handling and storage areas accessible to routine cleaning. Seal cabinets and kitchen equipment to the wall or floor, or have at least six inches of clearance to allow adequate cleaning. Kitchen equipment one to two inches off the floor or ¼ inch from the wall, is very difficult to keep clean and is usually an attractive site for cockroaches and other pests.

Locate food handling machinery to allow thorough cleaning. Cracks and crevices leading into voids often form insect breeding and harborage areas. Containers should be stacked on pallets. Leave aisles between stacked containers and walls for inspection and cleaning. Where practical, stack items 18 inches off the floor and 18 inches away from walls. This is called the "18 inch rule of sanitation."

Make sure that all doors and windows are tight fitting and that screens are provided on all windows and doors that can be opened. Screened doors should open to the outside. Take the nature of the surroundings into account when selecting construction materials.

Food handling and storage areas should be rodent proof and bird proof. Remember, mice can enter openings less than ¼ inch, and rats can enter openings less than ½ inch in diameter.

Remove waste food or garbage to proper storage or disposal sites at least daily.

Design a routine schedule for cleaning all areas. Some areas may need cleaning only once a week, others every day. In addition, spot clean spills and accidents.

When a new building is to be built, consult experts on the design and building materials to be used, since this is very important in a sanitation program.

Train maintenance personnel in sanitation. Many maintenance personnel forget to clean tools used in the offal room before using them in the processing or packaging area. If someone has to step on a conveyor belt to reach an overhead motor, make sure that it is cleaned afterwards.

A situation arose in one plant where management decided to close off the outside door of the box makeup room. To do this, they simply removed the door knob from the door, locking it shut. However, they forgot to fill in the hole the missing door knob created. This caused a 15/8 inch opening to the outside. Air was sucked in through the small opening into the box room and out into the main part of the plant. The opening was located adjacent to a dirty dock and dirt and debris were sucked in with the air. As a result of this, the shelf life of the product produced in that plant decreased by three days. This was just enough to begin spoilage and cause customers to complain.

Once the situation was recognized, a 15/8 inch plug was placed in the door and an exhaust fan was mounted in the wall to correct the air flow problem. The shelf life was regained. Indeed, very small items can cause very large problems. Screen or seal vent pipes, sewage lines, and other openings in walls and floors to prevent vermin entry.

The outside of the building presents the first impression of your operation to the public. Keep grass short, shrubs neatly trimmed and clean paved access ways. Maintain proper drainage to reduce or eliminate shelter areas for pests. Surround the building foundation with an 18 to 24 inch strip of 88 inch pebbled rock piled four inches deep in a trench. This discourages rodents from burrowing around buildings and keeps some turf pests from entering buildings. This makes an excellent area for traps and bait stations at food processing and storage facilities. If the bottom of the trench is lined with tar paper, weed growth will be retarded for a short time.

To reduce pest and vermin harborage, control weeds under fences or other barriers with various herbicides labeled for this purpose. Clean up all debris and trash. Store necessary supplies and equipment on racks at least 18 inches off the ground or on concrete slabs to reduce rodent and insect harborage.

Place garbage and food waste in enclosed containers that are emptied regularly. Containers should be off the ground on racks or on a concrete slab. Slope the grounds properly for adequate drainage. Poor drainage around buildings provides breeding places for insects (such as termites and cockroaches) and microorganisms (such as wood destroying fungi).

Locate outdoor lighting fixtures at a distance from buildings and aim them toward the buildings to help keep flying insects that are attracted to light away from doors and windows. You must instill in each employee the knowledge and desire to maintain cleanliness in a plant. Good housekeeping costs money, but poor sanitation costs more. Control over product quality begins with good sanitation today. There is no substitute for cleanliness and no excuse for its absence.

EXTRUSION TEHCHNOLOGY IN FOOD PROCESSING

Over the last few decades extrusion technology has played an increasingly important role in many industries such as food, feed and polymer. It has promising future. Extrusion is a multivariable unit operation i.e. mixing, shearing, cooking, puffing and drying in one energy efficient rapid continuous process. This process of High Temperature Short Time (HTST), extrusion bring gelatinisation of starch, denaturation of protein, modification of lipid and inactivation of enzymes, microbes and many anti nutritional factors. The extrudates are texturally and histologically restructured.

Considerable efforts had been put for developing high protein rich extrudate from various sources, such as fish live-stocks, microbial cells and oil seeds only. But high production cost and low efficiency of protein conversion by live stock make plant protein more suitable for dietary protein intake. Thus the present challenge to the food technologists and scientists is how to present nutritive ingredients in the form of recognizable food stuffs from cheaper easily available plant sources.

So the most plausible answer to use the newer food is characterized by its texture, which is determined by its micro-structure. Within technological limits the food technologist may control both the composition of starting material and processing variables to direct alteration for nutritional, textual and physical optimisation.

Extruders provide the most efficient means of converting electrical and mechanical energy into thermal energy for cooking feed and food formulations. The quality of an extruded product determines its success, failure, or product life. Extrusion processing parameters and ingredients influence the product quality. Extrusion processing variables that directly control product quality attributes are called independent variables. Changes made to independent variables affect the functional properties of the extrudates and process dates i.e. dependent variables as such.

Extrusion is a new equipment which is a continuous conveyor reactor. This could be used as mixer, heat exchanger, pressure vessel, reactor, shearing device, and expander. This tool is applied in product areas such as expansion at high pressure of products. Product profile :

- Infant food
- Dusoplings
- Pasta
- Instant beverage
- Pregelatinized starch
- 3-generation
- Cooked whole grains
- Snack foods
- Quick cooking vegetable
- Textured vegetable protein
- Biscuits/ Bread
- Break fat cereals
- Meat analogues
- Tortillas
- Precooked flour
- Pet food

— Food bars
— Precooked grits
— Vegetable protein treatment
— Structured proteins
— Crisp breads
— Bread sticks
— Animal feed
— Confectionery
— Croutons
— Byproduct treatment
— Frozen produce
— Instant noodles
— Meat products
— Butter/marga rine
— Reaction hydrolysis

Ordinarily cereal flours, tubers and their derivatives can be processed into snack food, breakfast cereals, confectionery items and precooked modified liquefied starches. Legumes and oil cakes based material can be transformed into texturized vegetable meat extenders, meat analogues.

Mixture of cereals and protein sources like legumes oilcakes can be transformed into ready-to-eat or semi cooked food with higher protein level. After oil extraction the meals can be heat treated by extrusion cooking in order to increase their nutritional value by denaturation of protein and or inactivation of antinutritional factor.

In most of the cases powered raw materials of a particular meshsize are used. The powdered raw material are then sent for separation of the fine dust. The powdered materials from blending mixture are tempered by adding predetermined amount of water and mixed thoroughly to adjust feed moisture content in between (15-25%).

The blending mixture are then allowed to equilibriate before extrusion. In general single screw extruder are used. The length to diameter ratio of the barrel is 20:1 and screw compression ration 1:1 to 1:4 is maintained. The extruder is provided with electrical brand heaters (over the barrel) and a temperature control facility.

In general the temperature of the feed and comparison zones are kept constant, while metering zones temperature varies from 120°C to 200°C depending upon the products. A screw operated feed hopper fed the extruder at a variable screw speed. The extrudates are collected when the operation is at steady state as indicated by smooth extrudate production and constant barrel and product temperature.

Extruded Aquatic Food Using

Extrusion-cooking is recognised as a basic technology in food and feed manufacture. Different food industries byproducts such as fish meal, groundnut cake, soybean cake, deoiled rice bran, soybean seed, fish oil with wheat flour and a binder were extruded in a single screw extruder to produce a semi-intensive aquatic food. The product quality was influenced by correct formulations of the products, proper processing conditions such as the particle size of the raw materials, moisture contents, feed rate, extrusion pressure, temperature and geometric design of the barrel, the screws and system locks. After a lot of trial the best result obtained by using a formulation containing 31% fish meal, 15% groundnut cake, 30 soybean cake, 11% soybean seed, 6% wheat flour, 5% deoiled rice bran, 1.75% fish oil and 0.25% guargum. The pulverized mixed raw materials size was minus 40 mesh and having 9% moisture content.

The food extruder is considered as a high-temperature short-time bio-reactor that transforms a variety of raw ingredients into modified intermediate and finished products. The advantage of extrusion are evident, especially in the simplification of processing techniques for the manufacture of existing products as well as in the development of new or novel types of food. Previously the technology was used in the manufacture of RTE cereals and snacks. In our country it is technology has not been fully exploited in the production of aquatic food with proper utilisation of some food industries byproducts namely fish meal, soybean cake, groundnut cake, deoiled rice bran, fish oil etc. with some starchy materials.

These products are cooked and formed on a single screw extruder at about 25% moisture. It is therefore necessary to dry down a moisture of 9-12% (wet basis). The product quality is influenced by extruder design, recognizable in physio-technological aspects such as residence time, shear type and level, degree of mixing, temperature development and thorough put. The present investigations were undertaken to develop a correct formulation based on food industries byproducts and to study the process parameters in the extrusion process. It will help a proper utilisation of food industries byproducts in a systemetic way.

All raw materials (Fish meal, ground nut cake, soybean cake, soybean seed, deoiled rice bran, wheat flour, guargum, fish oil) were procured from local market and analysed the proximate composition in the laboratory by AOAC methods. The initial laboratory analysis helped to achieve a correct formulation of the product. All the ingredients except wheat flour, fish oil and guargum were pulverized in an industrial pulverized and passed through a sieve of 40 mesh to a horizontal continuous mixer.

The wheat flour, guargum and fish oil were added directly to the mixer. The calculated volume of water was added to the mixer and mixed well for 30 minutes to get a desired level of uniform moisture content. The powdery materials were sent to extruder bin before extrusion then next to feeder.

Extrusion was performed on a single screw extruder (INOTEX-100, France). One circular die was fitted in the die plate having 0.5mm clearance. The feed rate was 18 kg/minute.

Food is one of the essentials for maintenance of life and is embedded in cultural and social habits of people. It is very important that the food available is safe/hygiene, wholesome with right nutritional content, free from infection/bacterial contamination, intoxication, contamination and adultration.

Changes have been brought about habits-resulting due to developments in technology and for socio economic reasons, food is in increasing demand for a range of food products. Therefore Food Regulations and standards have become a sensitive subject and the regulation of the quality of the food products the object of an increasing public interest.

Quality being the first consideration for the Consumer acceptance, which in turn is linked with recognised national and international standards, reflecting the national and international markets which are essential for the manufacturer to be able to design, produce and market products embracing the Consumer's needs of quality features and using upto date technologies. Complience with these standards is ensured through the use of regulatory standards and quality assurance systems.

Developments in Indian Food Processing Industry

In India, Food Science and Technology Education was initially masterminded by pure scientists in the field of chemistry, applied chemistry and bio-chemistry. The boderline between the basic science and technology and engineering was therefore not clearly demarcated at the initial stage. As a result, research projects that were undertaken in most of the premium food research institutions including Central Food Technological Research Institute (CFTRI) were designed on the line of basic science exploration in the areas of biochemistry, protein chemistry, nutrition and food processing. Those who have ventured into the processing and technology also focussed only on physio-chemical changes of food during processing and process parameters optimization.

Those who have ventured a little ahead thus incorporated process conditions standardisations to improve product quality. Nothing therefore happened in terms of any major breakthrough in process technology in India. The food research institutes including universities did very little in terms of technology upgradation and new product development which are of any commercial significance.

Whatever little we have seen in new product development and product quality upgradation is the result of the efforts on the part of the industry largely triggered from the need as a survival strategy in the face of competition. Some of these research institutions also suffer from the syndrome of reinventing the wheel. Crores of rupees have been spent by young food researchers reproducing the knowledge which are either known and or explored elsewhere. This therefore has put the industry, in particular and the nation, in general into the back gear.

Another factor that has marked the failure of food research activities in India to create any dent in terms of value addition in the processing and technology is due to the fact that there was little or no collaborative efforts between industry and research institutions. The mutual mistrust and lack of confidence on the part of the industry leaders on the ability of the institutional research to deliver value has increased with the passage of time. As a result, researchers have ventured into their own chosen subjects while industries have decided to go it alone.

Formation of an independent Ministry of Food Processing Industry which has now been reduced to the status of a department did not help change this scenario. The result is inevitable. While we can see a sea change in other industry categories in terms of product quality and value addition, in case of processed food industry changes are miniscule to say the least, and that too largely due to the efforts of the industry.

On the top of it, some of the premium institutions are in reality in a state of decay in terms of quality of research and education. The research activities that have been initiated earlier by the pioneers in food research and education have lost the inertia in the later years and thus died down. In the areas of research and education we now have a generation gap.

Liberalisation has brought in through the entry of large multinational and transnational corporations, foreign investment in this sector. This resulted in competition, technological upgradation and market expansion. In the face of the competition, domestic Industries are gradually losing market share and thus selling their businesses to the new entrant MNCs well before the value of the brand and businesses drops further due to ongoing onslaught of multinational brands. This is happening because MNCs have much greater resources to put behind their brand and business and also have long term vision and sustainability. Domestic industries are no comparison. The first attack came in soft beverages industry with Coke acquiring Parle brands and Pepsi acquiring Dukes and with the entry of Cadbury Schweepes in this sector entire soft drink industry is now in control of MNCs.

MNCs such as Nestle, Brooke Bond and SmithKline & Beechern controlled earlier only hot beverages (both white and brown segments). But soft beverage sector was dominated by domestic industries. With Coke and Pepsi acquiring Indian businesses, total non-alcoholic beverage industry is now under control of MNCs. Recently Sara Lee —a US multinational has acquired Nutrine—a large Indian bakery and confectionery business. Britannia is already under control of Danone group of France.

Only large bakery and confectionery left to be acquired in private sector is Parle Products. And with the entries of confectionery giants like Perfetti, Wriggly and Agrilimen confectionery and bakery sector, will also become the domain of MNCs.With Nestles' strong presence in Tomato Ketchup and Pickles and Hindustan Lever acquiring Kissan and Dipy brands from UB group through Brooke Bond route fruit and vegetable sector is also dominated by multinationals.

Heinz, the world's largest Tomato Ketchup manufacturer had acquired food business of Glaxo. Due to strategic restructuring of portfolio Glaxo decided to divest their dairy business with established brands like Complan, Glucon-D and Farex. Hindustan Lever, on the other hand, through a strategic alliance route, took control of Kwality Ice-cream as well as 100% Ice-cream brand of Jagatjit. Hindustan Lever with their own presence in dairy sectors, and with the introduction of Baskin Robbins and Walls has emerged as a dominant player in dairy segment, in general and Ice-cream segment, in particular.

Hindustan Lever (HLL) also acquired Dollop Ice-cream brand from Cadburys'. HLL, however, recently announced their intention to sell-off their Dairy unit in UP. Ice-cream industry, which is reserved for small-scale sector, has now been in the control of multinationals through a different route. The argument that ice-cream is actually a frozen dessert -- a nomenclature that has been accepted by both food and law ministry of Govt. of India -- paved the way for Hindustan Lever for this strategic acquisition. The earlier successful domestic businesses such as Dalmia Dairy, Foremost Industry and Jagatjit Industry in dairy sector are all in deep trouble—and MNCs have taken a control of this sector as well.

National Dairy Development Board (NDDB) with its strong brand Amul and with its deep root extended up to farmers level as a means of backward integration will of course, remains a significant force to reckon with. But nobody will deny that in branded dairy products Amul has to put up a constant fight against multinational brands. Vadilal is also a significant player in ice-cream but their presence is limited in Western India and for how long they will remain has to be seen. Kraft Foods a unit of Phillips

Morris is holding a licence to set up 100% owned entity and they are expected to come and set up their operation anytime.

In the convenience foods—'Corn Products', a US multinational is fast making progress. This is an old company, which did not make any significant contribution in the Indian food business largely because of lack of interest from their principals. CPC - International is now fast making progress with their well known Rex and Brown & Poison and Knorr soup brands. Recently they announced the acquisition of DCW Chemicals—makers of Captain Cook brands, which ran into rough weather because of the objection taken by some miller in Haryana to whom allegedly DCW has contractual obligations. Shortly, we will also have products in joint venture with Paoma Industries, the manufacturer of Rasna soft drink mixes and Campbell a world leader in canned foods.

Godrej, on the other hand, has joined hands with Pilsburry a leading player in the convenience foods business to boost their business activities. Filsburry has already introduced instant Cake mix. In this category others including Gits brand are relatively smaller and regional players. Apparently, first change that we have witnessed is of acquisitions of domestic brands in frontiers of food business by MNCs and alongwith although at a much lower scale a few joint ventures. Even the public sector undertaking, Modern Foods although making profit is up for sale in line with the Govt. policy of PSU disinvestment and ANZ Bank has been appointed to find a buyer for the same.

Ten years ago Indian processed food industries were crying about high taxation, lack of infrastructural support, nonavailability of quality raw material at competitive price, nonavailability of latest packaging machinery and packing material etc. as the major reasons for poor or sluggish growth of this sector. But the industry was still growing then, albeit not at the expected level. Competition was also there amongst domestic processors with their MNC counterparts. Because, large MNC food companies like Nestle, SmithKline Becheern, Britannia, Glaxo, Hindustan Lever etc. are there for ages. But domestic industries were not worried about their presence. There was healthy competition.

In some areas domestic industries were doing even better than some of their nearest competitors in multinationals. Why domestic industries are now not able to fight multinational giants? This is because the rules of the game have changed. Post liberalisation, we have now entered into an era of survival of the fittest. Only couple of years ago we had only Amul Cheese. Britannia first successfully introduced Cheese from cow milk followed by the introduction of French cheese 'Le'-Bon" from Dabur-Le'-Bon joint venture. Philips Morris—owner of Kraft Foods—is sitting waiting a formal licence to set up 100% owned company in India. They carried out lot of research for introduction of Kraft cheese in India. Their project now has been put in cold storage and they are still waiting and watching the market for processed food industry.

Upto mid eighties Kissan was the number one brand in Tomato Ketchup and around that time the competition came from Maggie—a Nestle's brand. With Maggie launching several varieties of Tomato Ketchup there was a growth in the market. With Kissan and Maggie fighting neck to neck other smaller but established brands like Dipy's from Herbertsons, Volfruit from Voltas, Noga of Nagpur Orange Federation and SunSip of Wimco gradually disappeared from the market. Delmonte now has joined hands with Paoma Industries, the manufacturers of Rasna Brands of soft drink concentrate and is expected to launch Tomato Ketchup shortly. The biggest global player in Tomato Ketchup Heinz is still waiting and watching. It was expected that they will launch Tomato Ketchup in Indian market soon. Some of the unknown local brands of course still existing only on price competition.

The price competition has also kept some of the other categories of food products still alive. For example, the age old Corn Flakes from Mohan Meakin under the brand name Champion still sells almost the same quantity (reportedly 500 MT per annum) against the much better quality Kellogs brand which sells around 300 MT per year with all its variants.

Till today we have only Parle and Britannia as two major brands in biscuits. Kellog is entering that segment gradually. Cadbury and SmithKline Becheem have nominal presence with speciality biscuits. In the snack foods category we have two successful Indian players namely Uncle Chips brand of Amrit Foods and Pepi of SM Dye Chem, others were local such as Fun Flip, Crax etc. Soon entered Pepsi with their Ruffles brand and soon extended to Indian snacks by introducing bhujjias which Bikanerwala makes for them to market.

In confectionery we have over half a dozen global players struggling here for brand share and fighting against Indian players like National, Norton, Parle, Parrys etc. Amongst MNCs in this field leading are Perfetti, Wriggley, Agrilimen, Park Davis. Competition is also seen in organised food retail chains. Couple of years ago we had only Narula running such an organised retail food chain. Today we have everybody namely. In some of these categories domestic brands are still a leader - for example,

Uncle Chips, Frooty, Rasna etc. But how long they will be able to retain their leadership is a big question mark? If, potato price continues to remain at the present level possibly Pepsi's Raffle will still continue even after incurring losses but Uncle Chip will have to close its shutters.

Technological Innovations

Food processing industry in India has undergone a total metamorphosis over the last six to seven years, in terms of types, variety, quality and presentation which is a result of liberalisation leading to foreign direct investment in frontiers of processed food sectors. Multinational and transnational corporations made significant contribution. This was possible due to market significant technological upgradation in this sector.

In seventies and eighties we used to talk about in seminars and conferences the new types of packaging, products and processes but industries never felt the necessity to upgrade or invest in new technology. Nor did they have the resources to support such programme. Reason was is the apprehension all around that there would be no market for such products. And we continued to produce products that are of traditional nature using age-old technologies. Besides, there would were licensing restrictions, reservation of many categories under small-scale sectors etc., resulting of into poor or negligible upgradation of the industry. Things have changed since then.

With the technological upgradation we now see an all round improvement in processed food products quality. The competition has forced the processors to improve and the upgrade the quality. Earlier we had limited categories, for example, jam, jellies, marmalades, squashes, cordials, ketchup and sauces in fruit and vegetable sector, ice cream, spray dried milk powder, condensed milk, butter and ghee in dairy sector, bread, biscuits and pancakes in bakery sector, hard boiled confectioneries, one brand and type of chewing gum and limited variety of chocolate in confectionery sector. Today we have not only better quality of these but also a lot of variants and product types and choices.

There is also a significant improvement in packaging quality. In seventies we had only glass and cans as packaging materials. In eighties we had seen laminates and other plastic materials coming in. Today we have the host of packaging types being used to market processed food products. Earlier we used to get fruit juices and ready-to-service (RTS) beverages only in glass bottles. Today we have tetra pack and also asceptic carton pack. Similarly, tomato paste earlier used to be sold in metal cans and the market for this was also very small.

Today tomato paste is sold by Godrej Foods in asceptic consumer pack. In packaging of cheese and other dairy products considerable improvement in the product and packaging quality are evidenced. Cheese, as a product was not known to the Indian consumer in seventies and eighties. Only cheese that we had was cottage cheese. Processed cheese was not there, not to speak of varieties of cheese as they are found and consumed in other countries.

Food items are primarily processed to extend its shelf life and to preserve its nutritional value. The secondary purpose of processing of food is to deliver convenience, taste and appeal to the target consumers. Depending upon what consumer segments we are targeting the processing methods, type of food and its taste and packaging and total presentation varies widely. In a country like India where local taste preferences differ from region to region it poses a much bigger problem to produce food products which can have a much larger acceptance and hence a bigger market potential.

But there are some food categories and types for which there is a universal acceptance and hitherto Indian processed food industry only were processing those generic category of foods for all India market. Even new entrants in the processed food industry were only adding brands in the traditional sectors. We have witnessed this phenomenon before liberalisation in different categories. And as a result, mortality rate of processed food brands were quite high. For example, when Amul came into the market with their Amul Butter - Polsons butter disappeared from the scene. And the successful brand went on extending it to other categories. Having tasted success, Amul brand has been extended across a range of items including cheese, cheese spread, shrikhand, chocolate and ice-cream.

Creativity in food industry was, to say the least, very low. There were of course small local companies who attempted to create products for catering to the local taste preferences but the market was so small that the products did not survive the test of time. For example Kissan launched "Bisebelle Bhath" a South Indian delicacy in Southern market in mid eighties only to withdraw a year later.

Before nineties the food industry in India was struggling to establish only the traditional food brands and there was very little or no effort to introduce new foods. In post liberalisation era we have host of new MNCs with superior marketing skill and bigger resource to their command have extended their brands to a wide variety of local foods and their variants including the areas which were protected niches of small local players. For example, Indian traditional snacks were only local brands even a couple of years ago. But there we have now even global brands. Kissan under UB-group used to sell and market only fruit and vegetable products.

Today Kissan brand has been extended to even branded grocery items which were earlier the domain of small local players. Pepsi's primary business is in soft drinks but in India they have gone into branding of traditional snack foods. Similarly Nestle - a swiss Food major - has introduced pickles in Indian market. In the traditional food items local companies should be able to add better value and hence can score higher in the market place.

In seventies, 'Bisleri' was the only mineral water which had national presence and the sale was to the tune of approximately one hundred thousand cases valued at about Rs.60 lacs. Today mineral water market is said to be of Rs.200 crores and over hundred brands of mineral water are there. Earlier we did not have any fruit juice in the market. Only canned juice and ready-to-serve beverages in bottles were available. Today we have number of brands in carton and tetrapack. Such as 'Onjus' of Enkay Texofood, 'Real juice' of Dabur, 'Jumpy' of Godrej etc. all packed in convenient asceptic cartons.

The proliferation of brands are also seen in branded Grocery products. A few years ago we had 'Tata-salt' as the only refined iodised salt selling in the market and today we have 'Captain Cook' from DCW, 'Kissan Annapurna' from Kissan Products and Catch (with dispenser) from Hi-Tech Foods and more brands to come in. In some areas such as meat and poultry products branding, packaging, processing and distribution on a national scale has yet to be witnessed.

But in many of the processed food categories, as we can see that the existing brand is either extended to a wide variety of foods such as Britannia to Cheese and Long Life Milk in tetrapack etc. or there are proliferation of brands. In this process, ultimate beneficiary is the consumer as they can expect to get the best value for their money. Competitive pressure will make that possible.

Mckensey did a study on the opportunity in India for food and agri business at the behest of Confederation of Indian Industries (CII). And as expected they projected a huge potential in food sectors and said that the real potential lies in traditional, local food and grocery items—but not so much in westernised processed food. Some of the big multinationals seem to have swallowed the Mckensey advise-pill and got into this sunrise sectors.

Historically, traditional food items were the domain of small local players. Grocery items earlier were sold loose and unbranded. Then some progressive traders started the cleaning, grading and primary packaging. And the next stage of development was branding of primary foods such as Atta (wheat flour), Rice etc. but those were mainly regional brands. Popular among these were "Rose" and "Shakti Bhog" brands in northern India.

Whereas in traditional food items such as spice and pickles there were host of local brands with regional strongholds such as 'Cookme' spice powder in East, 'Bedekar' pickles in West, 'MDH-masala' in North etc., to name a few. And the food ingredients —nobody thought of. Only food ingredient that was there was tomato puree and paste in cans which in the recent times Godrej introduced in tetrapack.

Edible oil in tin pack and later on in polyester jar and tetrapack were the first major step in branding grocery items. "Postman"—peanut oil from Ahmed Mills was one of the oldest popular brands. Today we get variety of edible oils and NDDB and Marico are the leading players in this sector. Amongst MNCs we have "Mazola" corn oil from CPC and "Sundrop" from ITC Agro—a sunflower oil which subsequently has been acquired by CONAGRA - the fastest growing food company in America. With CPC and CONAGRA being involved in edible oil market this sector is going to be soon dominated by MNCs.

The next major attempt to market a branded grocery item was done about a decade ago by Tatas by introducing the first refined iodised salt in poly bag by brand name "Tata Salt" and that was a success. The next big brand in this category is "Captain Cook" from DCW Chemicals who had plans in branded grocery items and thus the company introduced other items including wheat flour under the same brand name. But that was shortlived. During 1997 DCW Chemicals suffered a major setback and the company decided to divest this food business. The acquirer is Corn Products Co. (India) Ltd.—a wholly owned subsidiary of CPC-International a nine billion US dollar American multinational in food and grocery business. The company has recently changed its name to Best Foods Ltd.

CPC was a sleepy company operating in India for over fifty years and their performance was lacklustre. With their limited range of Rex and Brown and Polson brands of convenience foods, the parent company, although doing well globally did not have any commitment in India.

In post liberalisation era, this apparently sleepy company seems to have become active. The third brand of salt is "Kissan Annapurna" which is making a sustained effort to get market share. This brand which is now in Hindustan Lever's fold through Brook Bond acquistion who in turn acquired Kissan in early nineties have reportedly spent Rs.18 crores in advertising and got 14% market share in a Rs.200 crore branded salt category in a span of one year. Tata Salt still holds 26 percent market share and Captain Cook's share is about 20 percent and balance forty percent is still with the smaller players. With the acquisition of "Captain Cook" in branded salt market MNCs are the dominant players controlling sixty percent of the market.

The value addition in branded salt and pepper was really done successfully by a Delhi based local company Hi-Tech Foods belonging to Dharampal Satyapal of premium "Baba Zarda" (chewing tobacco) fame. Hi-Tech Food's `Catch' brand of salt and pepper in dispenser pack is a success story with upper middle class household and restaurant segments as the main customers. The sale of "Catch" is said to be around Rs.12 crores. The first MNC to get into the branded spice business was Brook Bond who introduced the select premium priced spice range by name "Sona" in late eighties. The products were priced and packaged for higher income group. They struggled for couple of years to establish "Sona" brand but failed and was forced to withdraw in later years. Apparently we don't see any major MNC in branded spice but world leader in exotic spices "Macomac" seems to have plan to enter Indian market.

The first MNC to introduce Indian pickles was Nestle with their Maggie brand. The products are still in the market. And as mentioned earlier, the first MNC to introduce traditional snacks (bujjias) is Pepsi under the umbrella of "Leher Namkins". It can be concluded that in traditional Indian foods MNCs cannot add much value through the involvement of their principals abroad. On the contrary, they will have to learn from the locals to derive advantage of their brand and resource muscle.

Hindustan Lever is expected to enter branded grocery items though Kissan route in a big way. The company does significant export of branded rice particularly in Middle East market and therefore expected to introduce the branded rice shortly in domestic market as well. Otherwise, in India so far branded packaged rice is limited to Basmati rice and there are many brands in this category and leading among them is "Kohinoor" — but all are from small manufacturers. The grocery business is basically low margins and high volume business and thus it required multiple supply source to be strategically located to reduce the cost of freight and excellent distribution infrastructure and logistics management capability. Big houses like HLL, therefore are expected to do much better in this sector.

In the food ingredients business MNCs have not yet traded. The only big player in this area is Dabur with their range of pastes such as onion, garlic, ginger and also mix of these for particular application. Current sales of these items which are sold under the umbrella brand "Hommade" is said to be Rs.5 crores and going by that standard it can be considered as a reasonable success. Very recently, "Cookme" curry paste has been launched in Calcutta. The market indicators point towards growth in the branded food ingredients business in coming years. Pepsi is expected to get into this category and with their backward linkages with farmers whom they support with the high yielding variety of seeds for better crop yield, it stands to have an edge over others in this sector. One could have expected that Nestle would also jump into the fray in this sunrise food business—but their new Italian Managing Director Mr. Carlo Donati seems to have other priorities and they want to focus on major key brands.

Price and quality are expected to be the major determinant in the success of grocery items and basic foods.

Consumers in India would not be willing to pay much as the price of convenience. Big global brands to MNCs' in that context are therefore not much of significance. Food retailing has come of age—from a period when food items were sold in small road side grocer shops & mandis and bazzars to a stage when food products are retailed through supermarket stores where consumers can inspect, select and pick up the products they like in a comfortable ambient and still pay a fair price for the product and the merchandise and sometimes even pay less than the price they would have paid at the nearest food stores.

Shopping foods is no longer a strenuous and uncomfortable affair. Instead, it is a pleasurable experience. From simple trading activity, food retailing is now graduating to a status of an industry. The first visible sign of the change in food retailing was seen in mid-eighties. Around that time a few new food stores were set up in all metro cities in India. Calcutta was the only exception where it started a little later. We had at that time couple of leading food stores started operating such as "Morning Stores" and "Modern Stores" in Delhi, "Nilgiri" in Bangalore, "Food Land" in Mumbai "Spencers Food Stores" in Chennai.

Food business analysts are of the opinion that food retailing will be changing and supermarket will soon be established in various smaller towns and thus food retailing industry has been predicted to be an in thing. To a large extent we can see that it is happening. Spencers were the first to tie up with a Singapore based large retail chain — "Dairyland" and had set up the food stores in Chennai. This was a technology tie up. The most crucial issue related to retail business is system and inventory management. A great deal of knowledge and experience are required in these areas in order to achieve ideal or optimum stock rotation and pricing for perishable and nonperishable foods and also for processed and fresh foods. Failing which one can lose money in the retailing business. In Mumbai, Garware group during late eighties had set up large food store which is now reported to have been closed down. But Food Land is still operating.

Prior to that, in cities like Mumbai and Delhi we had co-operative stores like "Apna Bazzar" in Mumbai and "Kendriya Bhandar" in Delhi. Both were very successful and are operating many outlets in all strategic localities in the city. When Escorts group was thinking in late eighties to diversify into non auto sectors which is their main business we deliberated a great deal and decided to get into agri business or food business. At that time MRTP provisions were restricting large group's entry in many industry sectors.

Today there are twenty food stores under "Nanz" operating in northern India alone—some directly owned and some are franchised. Today after eight years of the stores existance the company is still in the red. Some stores are making money but some are still losing. In India, particularly in metro cities the real estate cost is very high and to make a store of good size financially viable daily sales has to be minimum of Rs.1 lac which many stores could not generate. And as a result, like any other food industry the failure rate is very high here as well.

Oberio hotel group runs a few stores of processed and frozen meat and meat products including sausages, chicken drumstick, hotdogs etc. One such shop is located in Vasant Vihar in New Delhi. The product quality is comparable to what one gets in Europe or American stores. Although the process of development and growth of food retail stores might still be slow. But as we can witness today, the future is going in that direction.

Once developed, these food stores will become really a dominating trade partners for the food industry, who will be forced to give special discount and trade terms for them to get the shelf space in those successful food stores. Once established, the store label brands will become a real threat to the industry as manufacturers have to compete with the store label brands which are normally sold at a lower price. In Great Britain we have such big food stores namely "Sainsbury" and Tesco". Soon we are going to see either these stores in India or at least their equivalent.

Not too long ago for buying imported foods we had to go to select markets - such as Modern Bazar. Vasant Vihar in Delhi or Fort in Mumbai. In other places one has to literally search for such choice food items. In those days importing foods were not permitted. And we were told that these foreign made chocolates and soup mixes and cheese find their way to Modern Bazar through diplomatic routes in the sense that persons in diplomatic services bring with them these foodstuff and sell them to local stores.

But the fact of the matter is that these food items are brought to India through what is called "Suitcase trade" in the concerned circle. It will not take time for readers to understand what the "suitcase trade" is? It simply means to carry suitcase full of foodstuff by people frequently travelling overseas and selling and or delivering those to local traders and this happens in an organised manner. Those who can afford, have to pay a fancy price for those foreign foods. Although price was exhorbitant but the quality used to be distinctly better. Children love their Swiss chocolates, French Cheese and Italian pastas.

General Foods (now known as Kraft Foods International) - subsidiary of Phillips Morris has a synthetic orange beverage by brand-name "Tang" found to their dismay that so much of Tang is selling in India and Nepal now that they started thinking what would be the loss of sales to their South East Asian subsidiaries from where it finds its way to Indian market, once they start manufacturing it locally.

There are local agents who now represent many foreign companies and regularly import foods in turn to supply to local retailers and stores. In big stores like Nanz, there are regular requirement being catered to by their local agents. In earlier years we used to see these phenomena in countries like say in Middle East. This trade in imported foods will be on the increase as the custom duty goes down. It will also fuel the growth of partial processing in India to take the advantage of price equation. For example, importing the product in bulk and carrying out re-packing operation here will be more economical than importing the finished product itself.

As we know that India has now signed the WTO (World Trade Organization) agreement, of course, being a signatory to this agreement is a lesser evil than not signing it at all. As per the terms of reference to this agreement, by year 2003, India has to put most of the items under Open General License (OGL) for import which means these items can be freely traded. We so far could announce around about hundred odd items under OGL and in that list shrimp, strawberry, rasberry and other fruits, have already featured.

With the recent announcement of the Commerce Ministry, we have now freed import of 894 items including consumer goods and agricultural products by putting them under Open General Licence (OGL). Another 414 items are removed from the "restricted" list allowing these to be imported against Special Import Licence (SIL) that can be procured in the market by importers at a small premium.

Fruits like oranges and pomegranates, soft drink concentrates etc. are falling in SIL category whereas a range of marine food products, vegetables, assorted fruits and juices, spices, edible oils, jams, jellies etc. are brought under OGL.

The peak rate of the basic import tariff is now 40 percent which is applicable to most consumer products. On some items such as milk products India's WTO commitment bind it to a zero duty. But in most other agricultural products the WTO restriction is substantially higher ranging from 150 percent in the case of processed foods to 300 percent for edible oils. It is interesting to note that India, as a part of its globalisation policy is reducing the general tariff structure much faster than the asking rate as per WTO.

Quality Monitoring

In India, in the food and agriculture sector there are number of organisations responsible for the formulation of Standards and monitoring their quality. These can be generally classified in two systems as under.

— Compulsory Legislations

— Voluntary Standards

A Compulsory Legislations

Prevention of Food Adultration Act 1954

The most important compulsory legislation in our country in the area of Food Products is the Prevention of Food Adultration Act. (PFA-1954). The PFA-1954 Act is the basic Statutory regulation is intented to protect the common Consumer against the supply of adultrated food products.

The Act makes provision for prevention of adultration of food products and lays down that no person shall manufacture for sale, store, distribute any adultrated or misbranded food products not conforming to the Standards laid down under the Rules. These Standards are of minimum quality and are intended to ensure safety in the consumption of these food products and safe guarding against harmful impurities contaminations and adultration etc.

Provisions of this act are mandatory and contravention to these rules leads to both fine and imprisonment. The Central Committee for Food Standards (C.C.F.S.) and its various Subcommittees under the Directorate General of Health Services (D.G.H.S.) Ministry of Health and Family Welfare is responsible for operation and enforcement of the Act. Various interests concerned with Food Standards including consumer interests have representations in this Committee.

Essential Commodities Act 1954

A number of Control orders have been formulated under the provisions of the Essential Commodities Act. The main objectives of the Act are to regulate manufacture/ production, Commerce/trading and distribution of the essential commodities including the food products.

Some of the important orders of the act are enumerated below:-

The Fruit Products Order (F.P.O.-1955) The fruits products order regulates manufacture and distribution of fruits and vegetable products, sweetened aerated waters, ready to serve beverages, synthetic syrups, vinegars etc. The objective of the order is mainly to regulate, ensure the quality and hygiene of these products as per Standards laid down under the order.

The order is operated by the Ministry of Food Processing Industry through the Central Fruit Products Advisory Committee. The manufacture or relabelling of the fruits and vegetable products can be carried out only after a valid licence is issued by the Food Processing Ministry, which empowers the licensee to put their standard mark on the Food Products.

Solvent Extracted Oils, De-oiled Meal and Edible Flour Control Order, Vegetable Oil Products Order, Meat and Meat Products Control Order

These regulatory orders control the manufacture/ production and distribution of the products enumerated the objective being to ensure the quality and hygiene of these products as per various standards laid down in the order.

Solvent Extracted Act, De-oiled Meal and Edible Flour Control Order, Vegetable oil Products Order are operated by the Directorate of Vanaspati, Vegetable Oils and Fats. A licence for the production/manufacturing and distribution is necessary which is granted by the Directorate after on Satisfactory conditions being full filled.

Meat Food Products order is operated by the Directorate of Marketing and Inspection.

Voluntary Standards

The Voluntary Certification Systems in the food products is mainly organised by two bodies. The Bureau of Indian Standards (B.I.S.) is looking after the processed foods and their raw materials, while the Directorate of Marketing and Inspection AGMARK is looking after the standardisation of various raw and finished agricultural produce.

1. Bureau of Indian Standards (B.I.S.)

The main functions of the Bureau of Indian Standards the national standards Organisation of India are formulation of Indian standards for food and food products and their implementation by promotion and through voluntary and third party certification systems. These standards in general cover raw materials permitted and their quality parameters, hygienic conditions of manufacturing and product safety with respect of microbial Contaminations.

B.I.S. maintains and gives recognition to various laboratories for the purpose of standardisation and quality control. The B.I.S. Standard mark on the food products certifies that the product complies with a particular Indian Standard Specification and also guarantees that the manufacturer operates a quality assurance/control scheme in the production on a continued basis.

The Certification Scheme is basically voluntary but for some products of mass consumption affecting the health and safety of the consumer are brought under Compulsory/ Mandatory B.I.S. Certification Marking under various Act/ Rules and Notification of Government of India. The various products covered for mandatory B.I.S. certification are food colours and their preparations, food additives, preservatives, vanaspati, milk Products and infant foods.

2. Directorate of Marketing and Inspection (D.M.I.)

Directorate of Marketing and Inspection formulates grade Standards known as "AGMARK" with relevant quality definitions and grade designation marks in respect of various agricultural, horticulture, live stock, dairy and forest products. The quality of the product is assessed and determined with reference to various factors like different areas of production, variety, shape, weight, colour, moisture, fat content and other relevant chemical and physical parameters.

AGMARK grades are statutory grades expressed through AGMARK label/replica. These are framed under the provisions of the Agriculture Produce Grading and Marking Act and the General Grading and Marking Rules (1986 and 1988). Grading under the provision of this Act is voluntary but penalties for contravening the rules include fine, cancellation of manufacturing/production licence as well as imprisonment.

3. Eco-Mark

The Ministry of Environment and Forests have instituted on labelling of environment friendly products, on a national basis. With the consciousness of environment conservation growing day by day the adoption of ECO-MARK in different categories of food products will become necessary. The products will have to carry ECO-MARK a new standard certifying them environment friendly. The scheme provides to indentifying, accredation and labelling of consumer products which do least damage to the environment and also meet the quality standards/requirements of the relevant Indian Standard for the product.

Some of the food products identified under the ECO-MARK Certification are Tea, Coffee, Refined Vegetable oils, Vanaspati, Food Additives/Preservatives, Processed Fruits and Vegetable Products, Infant Foods and Beverages.

4. ISO Standards

With the increasing focus being given to the management of quality worldwide, the International Standards

Organisation has introduced the quality system standards ISO 9000 series. These Standards provide guidelines and criteria for the formal control of products and services by the manufacturing company and assure the purchaser/consumer a consistent acceptable standard of products and services. ISO Standards reflects a long term concepts and terminology, quality systems and supporting technologies.

Implementation of Standards/Quality Control

For effective implementation of the regulatory standards and monitoring the quality of the graded and certified foods and food products made available by the manufacturers requires a net work of Testing/Analytical Laboratories with basic modern analytical facilities and technical manpower.

The functions of these laboratories will be:

— To carry out/undertake the testing of the food products as per various regulatory standards and ascertain their compliance to the relevant standards.

— Undertake Research and Development (R&D) investigations, Collaborative Studies and generation of data for evolving new standards and revising the existant standards and quality assessment studies.

— To identify and take corrective actions on non-conformities observed by quality assessments.

Before undertaking the testing of Food Products it is necessary to classify the Foods Products and the quality tests to be undertaken. Food and Food Products are classified as under:

— Sugar and Honey Products.

— Edible Starches and Starch Products.

— Food Grains and their Products.
— Bakery and Confectionery.
— Protein Rich Foods.
— Spices and Condiments.
— Fruits and Vegetable Products.
— Stimulant Foods like Tea, Coffee, Cocoa Powder.
— Alcoholic Drinks and Carbonated Beverages.
— Dairy Products.
— Meat, Fish and Poultry.
— Oils Fats and Oil Seeds.
— Food Colours, Preservatives, Additives.
— Snacks, Fast Foods, Cooked Foods.
— Physical Parameters

Specific gravity/density, Refractive Index, Butyro-refractometer leading, Polarisation/Optical Rotation Refractions like foreign matter inorganic/organic, Colour.

Issues in Colouring of Food Products

An attractive colour is associated with quality and freshness. Consumers have expectations with regards to the typical colour of certain foods. A non attractive colour makes a product look as no longer fresh and likely to be rejected. We eat with our eyes, in most cases we do not enjoy food which does not match our colour perceptions. Colour has important psychological implications it particularly true in case of food. The initial perception of food by consumers is visual.

Therefore colour has a very important role and the acceptance or rejection of a food product often depends on it. An attractive colour is associated with quality and freshness. Consumers have expectations with regards to the typical colour of certain foods. A non attractive colour makes a product look as no longer fresh and likely to be rejected. The eyes also play an important role in the actual eating process. Therefore it is very important to conserve the characteristic colour of a food product as far as possible during manufacturing and storage.

One example is bread, which is generally perceived as golden brown. A golden brown crust is important visually and definately enhances flavour. Pale bread has neither the same sales nor the same appetite appeal. Colour of bread is directly related to the colour of the pans in which it is baked. Unless new pans are factory prepared, their light coloured exteriors reflect oven heat away from the dough. The result is pale, poorly flavoured bread. It is not until pans have been used repeatedly that their exteriors darken, consequently absorbing oven heat, which is immediately transmitted to the dough creating the right crust colour and flavour.

Colouring of food products is required:

— To replace colour lost during preparation (e.g. preserved fruits and vegetables);

— To makeup the colour of a product whose ingredients cause it to become fade (e.g. sauces and drinks);

— To ensure consistent colour of products (e.g. confectioneries and desert products);

— To render the characteristic flavour more recognizable (e.g. synthetic syrups).

— Technical Possibilities for Colouring Food Products:

— Through the addition of colourant foods (e.g. Beetroot).

— With natural colouring agents occurring in food (e.g. Beta - carotene).

— With natural colouring agents not occurring naturally in food (e.g. Caramine).

— With permitted synthetic food colours.

— With inorganic pigments.

— Colourant Foods

The main colourant foods are beetroot, paprica extract, turmeric, grape juice and juices of coloured berries etc. These colourants have weak colouring effect and can also produce undesired flavours. Finally the poor colour stability restricts their use for colouring of food products.

The natural colouring agents are chlorophyll, anthocyanin, carotenoids, riboflavin, curcumin, betanin, and cochineal (obtained from Cochineal Insect). In many cases these are not sufficiently stable to heat and light and at certain pH levels.

Synthetic Dyes: These do not occur in nature and have to be manufactured artificially. These are patrochemical product that can be made in practically unlimited quantity and with a high degree of purity, intensive colour concentration and consistent quality. These are resistance to heat, light and chemical influences.

Methods of Colouring

If food needs to be coloured for any of the reasons mentioned above, and if this cannot be done using coloruing foods, the first step is to decide which colouring agents are allowed by law for the product in question and in what quantities. It depends on the properties of the food. The stability and possibility of interaction between colouring agent and food ingredients must also be borne in mind, as is the exposure to heat in manufacture and/or processing by the consumer, and the packaging and storage conditions, including possible light influences. At all events, preliminary experiments and stability test should be carried out. Labelling obligations should also be considered and discussed.

FOOD LAWS

In India, Prevention of Food Adulteration Act 1954 define colouring matter as under:

Rule 23: Unauthorized addition of colouring matter prohibited. The addition of a colouring matter to any article of food except as specifically permitted by these rules, is prohibited.

Rule 24: Extraneous addition of colouring matter to be mentioned on the label - Where an extraneous colouring matter has been added to any article of food that shall be written on the label attached to any package of food so coloured a statement in capital letters as below.

Rule 25: Use of caramel permitted — Not with standing provisions of Rule 24 (and Rule 32 (c) caramel may be used without label declaration.

Rule 26: Natural colouring matters which may be used — Except at otherwise provided in the rules the following natural colouring principles whether isolated from natural colors or produced synthetically may be used in or upon any article of food.

— Beat-carotene

— Beta-apo-8-carotenal

— Methylester of Beta-apo-8' carotenoic acid

— Ethylester of Beta-apo-8' carotenoic acid

— Canthaxanthin

— Chlorophyll;

— Riboflavin (Lactoflavin)

— Caramel

— Annorto

— Saffron

— Curcumin (or turmeric)

Rule 27: Addition of inorganic matters and pigments prohibited—Inorganic colouring matters and pigments shall not be added to any article of food: (Provided that chewing gum may contain Titanium dioxide — Food grade up to a maximum limit of 1 per cent.

Rule 28: Synthetic food colours which may be used — No Synthetic food colours or a mixture thereof except the following shall be used in food.

Rule 29: Use of permitted synthetic food colours prohibited — Use of permitted synthetic food colours in or upon any food other than those enumerated below is prohibited:

— Ice-cream, milk Iollies, frozen deserts, flavoured milk, yoghurt, ice-cream mix powder.

— Biscuits including biscuit wafers, pastries, cakes, confectionery, thread candies, sweets, savouries (dal moth, mongia, phululab, sago papad, dal biji only);

— Peas, strawberries and cheries in hermatically sealed containers, preserved or processed papaya, canned tomato juice, fruit syrup, fruit squash, fruit cordial, jellies, jam, marmalade, candied crystallized or glazed fruits;

— Non-alcoholic carbonated and non-carbonated ready-to-seve synthetic beverages including synthetic syrups, sherbets, fruit bar, fruit beverages, fruit drinks, synthetic soft drink concentrates;

— Custard powder;

— Jelly crystal and ice candy;

— Flavouring agents and soup powder.

Rule 30: Maximum limit of permitted synthetic food colours—the maximum limit of permitted synthetic food colours or mixture thereof which may be added to any food article enumerated in rule 29 shall not exceed 100 parts per million of the final food or beverage for consumption, except in case of food articles mentioned in clause (c) of rule 29 where the maximum limit of permitted synthetic food colours shall not exceed 200 parts per million of the final food or beverage for consumption.

Rule 31: Colours to be pure — The colours specified in Rule 28 when used in the preparation of any article of food shall be pure and free from any harmful impurities.

In European Union, Directive 94/36/EC on colours for use in food stuffs — This directive was drafted as a response to the continued need for food colouring in a single marked calling for the free movement of goods and fair competition, coupled with the demand for consumer protection and health safety. It stated in particular that all unprocessed food stuffs and certain other basic foods should be free of additives, and also set out strict provisions concerning the use of additives in food for babies and small children.

The directive defines colours as substances that give or restore colour to food. It includes natural ingredients of foods and natural raw materials that are normally used neither as food stuffs nor as typical food ingredients. Preparations made from food stuffs and other natural raw materials obtained by selective physical and/or chemical extraction of the nutritional or aromatizing components of pigments are also regarded as colours within the meaning of the directive.

Foodstuffs, whether dry or in concentrated form, and flavouring substances which are added during the manufacture of food preparations for their aromatizing, flavouring or nutritional properties and which have an incidental colouring effect — such as paprika, tumeric and saffron — are not regarded as colours. Nor are those in parts of the food such as cheese rinds and sausage skins that are not intended for consumption.

Betanin obtained from beetroot or anthocyan extracted from red grape skin, for example, are regarded as colouring agents rather than colouring foods. The colours themselves and their aluminum lakes are treated in the same way. There are some colours in the EU list that are not contained in all national colour lists or that are subjected to restrictions in Germany. Some technically insignificant carotenoids no longer figure in the list.

The caramels differ in terms of manufacture and application:

— E150a plain caramel, alcohol-stable, for spirits and confectioneries

— E150b caustic sulfite caramel, alcohol-stable, for spirits

— E150c ammonia caramel, for beers, soups and sauces

— E150d sulfite ammonia caramel, acid-stable, for non-alcoholic carbonized drinks.

Additive regulations in Germany and other countries used to contain a positive list of foodstuffs that could be coloured. A product that did not figure in the list could not be coloured. Exceptions were made at the time for riboflavin, carotene, and in some cases for caramel. This special status has now been abolished.

The maximum levels refer to readymade food products prepared as instructed, and to the quantities of basic colouring components in the colouring additives. For example, E104 quinoline yellow may be used in confectioneries up to a maximum of level of 300 mg/kg. Commercial E104 quinoline yellow contains 70% pure colour, so that a maximum of 428.6 mg/kg of this agent may be used, as the thresholds refer to the colour-giving component only.

With quantum satis references there is no maximum level. It is expected, however, that the colours will only be used to the extent necessary to achieve the desired aim. The consumer may not be misled.

In Germany, C colours, e.g. methyl violet (C2), are allowed for stamping eggs and meat. All colours of this type are not fobidden. Only E155 brown HT, E133 brilliant blue FCF, E129 alua red AC, or a suitable mixture of E11 brilliant blue FCF and E129 allura red AC are allowed for labelling meat products.

Colours E123 amarnath, E127 erythrosine, E128 red 2G, E154 brown FK, E160b annatto, E161g canthazanthin, E173 aluminum and E180 lithol rubine BK may not be sold directly to consumers. This is a protective measure given the low ADI (acceptable daily intake) of these substances.

Despite some weaknesses, the directive represents a major advance for European food manufacturers and considerably facilitates the exchange of coloured foodstuffs within the EU.

Labelling of food colouring agents

When labelling food coloring agents a distinction has to be made between:

— labelling of the container in which the colourant is delivered to the food manufacturer and

— labelling of colorants on food packaging.

The latter is of significance for the consumer: no distinction is made in the declaration between the use of natural, nature-identical or artificial colours. With pre-packed products the colours in the list of ingredients must be identified as such followed by their commercial name or E number. For colourant foods the commercial name is sufficient.

Unpacked and pre-packed food exempt from the requirement for an ingredient list must be indicated "with colour". If the pre-packed food comes with a list of ingredients, this indication is not required.

Quality Assurance

Suitability should be tested before colours are used on an industrial scale by comparing the appearance of a freshly coloured food sample with samples made using a different formulation and stored either in original or comparable packaging for a defined period e.g.

— next to window at room temperature

— in a warming cabinet without light at 35-40 DC

— under artificial light without heat, or

— heated close to a lamp (40-50 cm)

Quality Control

Quality control of coloured product is often carried out by comparing a sample with standard. Spectrophotometry is used a major the color of liquid and transparent product. The measurement takes place in a visual spectrum range. For non-transparent or insoluble product colour is measured by calculating the colour coefficient on the basis of the standard light reflected from the product:

— Analysis can be performed in two ways:

— Isolation of the colour from the food and subsequent investigation.

— Investigation of the colour present in the product.

As identification of a food colour involves only a few substances and reference material is normally available, either in pure form or as part of mixture, simple paper or thin-layer chromatography can be used. With isolated colours it is also possible to compare their reaction with acids and alkalis, of their solubility in concentrated sulfuric acid and subsequent changes in color when diluted with water. Quantities (intensity, mixing ratio) can most easily be determined by spectrophotometry. Inorganic pigments are identified by classic reaction tests. Colour coatings are measured after dissolution in dilute hydrochloric acid.

Sugar is the most popular sweetener in the market. It also possesses preservative, bulking, flavour enhancing and texturing properties. The major reason for its popularity are its ready availability, low cost, simplicity of production, purity and long history of usage. If hydrolysed, it produces invert syrup which manifests the above properties by many folds. Innovation is the key to success. Innovation needs to be persuaded vigorously for the upgradation of technology so that transformation in product quality and betterment of life are achieved.

A breakthrough innovation has been achieved in the field of sweetener through biotechnological production of invert sugar (IS). A radical change in the quality of food and pharmaceutical products has been achieved by replacing sugar with invert sugar. The technology has revolutionised the market in such a way that new industrial units are being set up to meet the diversified application of invert sugar. R and B activities are also being carried out.

Sugar is the most popular sweetener in the market. It also possesses preservative, bulking, flavour enhancing and texturing properties. The major reasons for its popularity are its ready availability, low cost, simplicity of production, purity and long history of usage. If hydrolysed, it produces invert syrup which manifests the above properties by many folds. Although, this information was known, no industrial unit for IS production was started in the country due to the absence of proper technology.

The old age method of acid inversion was the main tool for IS and few actual users adopted this technique for their requirement. This old age method is crude, results non uniform products including formation of highly neuro toxic hydroxy methyl furfural (HMF) and furfural. The above crude acid hydrolysis can be improvised by ion exchange resin. The uniform product quality is obtained by adopting this method. Most of the manufacturers in the world use the resin technology for IS production. However, the main constraints of the process are operational difficulties, above 45% sugar solution leading to blockage of flow, high cost of resin, carbonisation, high degree of effluent generation and formation of HMF.

The said coversion can also be achieved by enzymatic action of invertase on sugar. Enzyme being target oriented and mild in nature, does conversion with almost same percentage efficiency without any byproducts formation. However, for commercial success of the process, it is necessary to immobilise a cheap source of invertase for its repeated use and by utilising concentrated sucrose solution to avoid upstream and down stream processing.

A number of attempts have been made to produce IS using immobilised enzyme route. Most of the reported work failed to see the ray of light of commercialisation for a number of reasons particularly the absence of cheap right quality food grade, immobilised system having high biocatalytic activity and stability under practical operating conditions. A commercially viable technology has been developed by Food Technology Department of Bhabha Atomic Research Centre to produce concentrated IS by a single step biocatalytic process from concentrated aqueous solution of sucrose.

The substrate sucrose is passed through bioreactors containing immobilized invertase. Yeast cells (S. cerevisiae) are used as source of enzyme invertase, tailor made to obtain the maximum biocatalytic activity of the enzyme and then immobilized in an inexpansive inorganic matrix. The matrix used is very cheap, easily available, inert, has high mechanical strength, density and possess high thermal and dimensional stability. The matrix is resistant to microbial attack and nontoxic. The bioreactor once packed can be used continuously for several months (6-8 months). The product conforms to the BP standards and is absolutely free from HMF and thus absolutely safe for use. The process is virtually maintenance free and simple in operation. It does not create any problem of pollution or effluents and absolutely free from hazards.

The process was scaled up from bench scale level of 3 Kg/day to 500 Kg/day commercial plant leading to successful scale up to 10 MT/day. A number of industrial units are operating based on the technology. The product finds numerous applications. The process is first of its kind in the world commercialised for the production of invert sugar based on whole cell immobilisation of yeast cells.

IS is 1.3 times sweeter than sugar and, therefore the quantity used for sweetening any item is greatly reduced. It tastes like honey and therefore can be used as a substitute for honey. As it is available in a ready-to-use liquid form, the problem of storing is minimised. It is free from dental carioneity (commonly known as dental caries) because of its unique property of not reacting with body calcium, restricting the formation of dental caries. It is a natural preservative, and has a longer shelf life.

It does not produce off-odour or off-taste when stored for a long period of time and used in higher concentration. It does not crystallise at high concentration and lower temperatures, thereby minimising crystal formation in ice-cream. It caramelises at lower temperature, thereby reducing the baking temperature from 350 degrees to almost 200 degrees, and giving a rapid crust colour. It assimilates faster in the stomach as compared to ordinary sugar. It has a higher degree of solubility than sugar. It has higher osmotic pressure than sugar. It maintains the calcium balance in the body.

IS is better than other sweeteners that are often used, like saccharine, cyclamate and aspartame because of the quality of sweetness and also because it does not produce off-flavour at high usage levels. Its use leads to formation of spongier cakes and ice-cream devoid of crystals, crispier and evenly baked biscuits without cracks, caramalisation at a lower temperature and therefore, reduced time taken to bake cakes. IS is India's answer to Europe's High Fructose Corn Syrup (HFCS), a substitute for sugar. IS is finding new application in the fields of tobacco, face cream, shoe polish etc.

Initial market data shows that there is a tremendous growth potential of the product particularly in view of the changed economic, scenario of our country. Indian manufacturers can compete in international market by adopting the technology invented in the country (single step) which is superior and cheap to multi steps HFCS technology. Moreover, in India, production of sugarcane, a plant that fixes more carbon then corn is abundant and thus scope for production of invert sugar through inversion is the most appropriate choice of technology

High Fructose Syrup

One of the major discoveries in the field of nutritive sweeteners was the development of a process for the isomerization of glucose to fructose. For the first time it became possible to produce a starch derived syrup which was as sweet as sucrose (sugar) and known as 'High fructose syrup' (HFS) which has become a major sweetener with in two decades. The shift to sucrose is akin to the shift from honey to sucrose in the middle ages. The shift was catalysed by the economic incentives provided by the wide fluctuations in sugar prices (in the United States) and a desired to develop an alternate sweetener from abundantly (in the U.S.A.) available maize.

The genesis of fructose syrup

Sucrose has been man's primary sweetener. Sucrose is sweeter than glucose, and pure crystals can be recovered from juices extracted from sugar beets or sugar cane with relative ease. The higher sweetness of sucrose as compared to glucose prevented the latter from capturing only a small fraction of the sugar market. When sugar is hydrolyed with a 50:50 invert syrup is produced. The starch industry aimed to be able to produce such a syrup by the isomerization of glucose to fructose as this would mean an additional avenue for maize utilization. In the USA this is considered to be another avenue for the use of corn.

The degree of enzymatic isomerization depends on several operating parameters. While isomerization levels in excess of 50% fructose are possible, conversion to 42% fructose content was selected as having the best balance between increased sweetness and process economics. The first commercial shipment of 42% fructose syrup was made in 1968.

The new sweetener did begin to replace sucrose in many applications. However, it was not sweet enough to meet the demands of the soft drink producers. A separation procedure was developed that was able to produce a syrup with over 90% fructose. This syrup is blended with 42% syrup to produce a syrup with 55% fructose, acceptable to soft drink manufacturers.

Within a few years fructose syrup represented more than half of the caloric sweeteners consumed in the U.S.A. By the late eighties there were over 80 manufacturing units worldwide, producing more than 6.6 million MT (dry basis) of fructose syrup. The use of HFS in food processing industry became so extensive that both 'Pepsi and 'Coke' switched over to 100% HFS in place of surcose. In the USA, starch based sweetners have capatured 60% of the sweetner market.

The growth of the HFS market is linked to the availability of sugar, especially in countries like India, who are major sugar producers. It is therefore, necessary to briefly review the sugar scenario. Apart from Asia there has been a slow consumption growth for sugar. One factor has been a significant volume of high fructose corn syrup (HFCS) substituting for sugar in North America and some Asian countries such as Japan.

However, despite rapid growth in sugar consumption, Asia continues to have the lowest sugar consumption of any region. For the world's two most populous nations, India and China, sugar consumption in 1995/96 is projected at 15.0 and 8.0 millions MT, up 3.4 and 1.9%. With a combined population in 1994/95 estimated at 2.2 billion, India and China are expected to account for nearly 60% of Asia's total sugar use and nearly 20% of the world total.

A decade earlier, India's sugar use was estimated at 9.1 million and China's at 2.2 million tons-together only 11.5% of the world total. Per capita sugar use for India is now around 14 kilograms and for China only 6 kilograms, strikingly different from the 30 to 40 kilogram range in Europe and much of Latin America.

India is near the bottom of the list when it comes to soft drink consumption. Most sugar in India is used in hot beverages such as tea and coffee, and in traditional confections. The demand for sweeteners in India is expected to increase, and one of the areas that could see considerable growth is soft drinks. This is an area that is the largest user of HFS worldwide, and the CII-McKinsey & Company FAIDA study, January, 1997, drinks are in the large market size, high growth rate area.

There are three main constraints to the manufacture of HFS in India. The first is the cost of manufacturing HFS vis-a-vis the price of sugar. The second is the availability of maize. The third are the provisions of the Prevention of Food Adulteration Act, 1954 and other relevant laws. Regarding the cost of manufacture, it should be noted that the comparison of costs should be between HFS and the price of sugar solution after purification, as used by the soft drink industry. Also, if the demand for HFS and other starch applications grow, the amount of maize processed will increase, and the economies of sale will bring the cost of manufacturing starch down.

The newer plants which will be necessary to handle the increased volumes will be more efficient than existing plants. The international norms for recovery are much higher than those prevailing for most plants in India. For example, starch yields can be as high as 67% in the United States. In India, they are usually less than 64%.

Based on these criteria a detailed investigation is being undertaken to access the viability of producing HFS in India. Regarding the availability of maize, prima facie, it would appear that it should be possible to increase production more easily than the production of sugarcane. The yield of maize in India is a low 1.5 MT per hectare compared to a world average of about 3.6 MT per hectare and a high of 8MT per hectare in the United States, Canada, and Western Europe. With the proper inputs it should be possible to double production in a relatively short time much in the manner that the "green revolution" increased the availability of wheat in India. Regarding PFA, there is no mention of high fructose syrup of fructose. The Fruit Products Order, 1955, permits the use of "invert sugar fructose" under Part II. A sine-qua-non for any enterprise starting the manufacture of HFS would be an unequivocal indication that the law permits its use in various applications.

Directorate General of Health services, P.H. (Food) Section, Government of India, should, on it own, go ahead with ammending the provisions and listing HFS as a sweetening agent under Rule A.07 of Appendix B, and also permitting its use in products for which a standard of identity exists. The world-wide acceptance of HFS as a food additive and sweetening agent, as well as the fact that its constituents are permitted in foods, should not make this difficult.

Self-Supporting Edible Films

Edible films are defined as a thin layer of edible materials formed on food as a coating or a self-supporting thin layer placed (pre-formed) on or in-between the food components, and in both cases consumed along with the food. Though edible films in the form of coatings are traditionally used to extend the shelf life of food and maintain its quality by inhibiting the migration of moisture, oxygen, carbon dioxide, aromas and lipids, development of the self-supporting form has been the subject of tremendous research since the last decade. The worldwide interest on such films is evident from increasing number of publications mentioning various properties of the developed films.

The self-supporting films have been prepared by casting solutions of proteins, carbohydrates and lipids, in different combinations and compositions. Their properties are found to be affected considerably by different factors at different stages in the process. Table 1 gives a comprehensive view on this aspect. The raw materials those have received attention include polysaccharides (e.g., cellulose, modified cellulose, starch, agar, carageenan, alginate, pectin, dextran, pollulan, curdlan, etc.), proteins (e.g., zein, gluten, collagen, gelatin, ovalbumin, myofibrillar proteins, etc.) and lipids (e.g., carnuba wax, bees wax, lauric acid, palmitic acid, stearic acid, etc.).

The properties of the edible films those have been mostly evaluated are mechanical properties, like ultimate tensile strength (UTS) and percent elongation at break (EL) and the barrier properties, like water vapour permeability (WVP) and oxygen permeability. Although most of the developed films show desirable oxygen permeability, their moisture barrier and mechanical properties are poor in comparison to the synthetic polymeric films5-7.

Inclusion of lipids in the film in emulsified form or following the technique of formation of a composite bilayer has been found to improve the moisture barrier property of the films8. Nevertheless, the mechanical strength of the edible films appear to be quite reasonable for making casings, wrappers or using as a septum in some heterogeneous fabricated food items. In addition to their usefulness as edible coatings when applied externally, self-supporting films, can control the diffusion of different ingredients from one part to other within the food when applied as a septum in between the layer of a fabricated heterogeneous food.

Additionally, self-supporting edible films can carry antioxidants, antimicrobials in very specific area of a multicomponent food system without unnecessarily incorporating the same throughout. Traditional packaging materials can not compete in these aspects. Self-supporting edible films can conveniently be used as wrapper for low moisture and confectionary items. Films with considerable mechanical strength could be used for making small pouches.

In food packaging usually multibarrier functionality is needed which is normally achieved with the help of a laminated multilayer synthetic package. Such disposed packages are difficult to recycle and ultimately become a potent pollutant to the environment. Pouching of foods with edible film will definitely contribute its inherent barrier capacity and convert the need of conventional multilayer laminated packages to simpler, even a single layer synthetic package; the edible pouch could be used as a part of the food, if liked, or as feed.

Although the concept of total replacement of synthetic packaging materials remains doubtful, such simplification will certainly reduce the consumption of the petroleum-based raw materials to a considerable extent. Moreover the simplified synthetic package, if it is a single layer one could conveniently be recycled. More important practical aspect is the prevention of environmental pollution through the reduction of the amount of synthetic plastic in the package disposal.

Additionally, when fabricated from highly dissolvable material, self-supporting films could be used for making instant soluble pouches for soup mix, flavouring components, leavening agents, etc. Such packets get dissolved in the mix and could release the contents just at the time of mixing. Ideally, there is no need to dispose off the package. Thermoforming, overwrapping, and shrinkwrapping of foods with self-supporting edible films is also conceivable.

On a broad perspective, edible films (which are otherwise completely biodegradable too) with appreciable mechanical strength could also find applications as packaging materials or wrappers for some non-food items for protection from various environmental contamination during their handling, storage and distribution. Thus, the favourable aspects of edible films can be summarised as follows.

(1) The films are completely biodegradable.

(2) The films can be a part of a food/used as feed.

(3) The films can reduce the consumption of naphtha-based polymeric films

Therefore, development of edible films with good mechanical and barrier properties is undoubtedly a challenge in the modern food science. Information on commercialisation has recently been available with the film made from hydroxypropyl cellulose. These films are used to form pouches that allow processors to add pre-measured amounts of additives such as colorant and vitamin pre-mixes directly without further handling.

Although this developmental work is very active at the international level, this is still at a rudimentary stage in India. Since recent past, some scientist at Post Harvest Technology Centre, IIT, Kharagpur, is persuading on the development of starch-based edible films. The films are quite appealing in appearance; their mechanical and moisture barrier properties are comparable to many reported protein-based edible films. Recently, one work has been published9 on development of edible film from shark meat by the scientists working at Bhaba Atomic Research Centre.

Nutritional Foods

Consumers are exposed to a whole range of processed foods everyday. Those who do not want the inconvenience of preparing their own meals are willing to pay a premium for foods perceived to be of high quality and standard. One of their main bases of comparison is the information on the labels of these items. But our foods regulations in India are not elaborate and stringent enough to make it mandatory for the manufacturers to declare relevant information on the label to guide purchase decisions of the consumers.

In United States a regulation related to nutrition labelling was passed in 1973 but compliance was entirely voluntary unless nutritional claims were made or nutrients are added in the food products intended for sale. Although it was a voluntary declaration, manufacturers in United States and in other developed countries were complying with the requirement because of competitive pressure.

In 1990 Nutrition Labelling and Education Act (NLEA) was passed and as a consequence it is now mandatory that all foods marketed in the US market must carry nutrition information in a standardised format. Also to encourage judicious purchase decision by the consumer, the information must indicate how the food contributes to a healthy diet. The regulations are result of the growing health and nutrition consciousness of the typical American consumer. A food and Drug Administration (FDA) survey this year showed that 55 percent of American consumers made their decisions based on what appeared on the panel. Similar survey in Australia showed that four out of five read food labels when make purchase of food items. Other consumer surveys have shown that well over half the shoppers worldwide are scanning the labels on food products.

The standard format called 'Nutrition Facts' must indicate according to the new Act, per serving size, total calories, calories from fat, saturated fat, cholesterol, sodium, total carbohydrates, dietary fibre, sugars, protein, vitamin A, vitamin C, calcium and iron. For easy understanding, the values are generally given in grams for each nutrient and as a percentage of recommended daily allowance to help the consumer not only compare food quality for various alternatives available but also to decide the daily food intake to meet the daily dietary nutrition requirement. This helps to maintain consumers health and promote nutrition education.

As against that scenario in India we have a prevention of Food Adulteration Act (PFA) and to regulate processed fruit and vegetable product we have Fruit Products Order (FPO). While PFA comes under Ministry of Health, FPO falls under the purview of Ministry of Food Processing Industry (earlier this was under Ministry of Agriculture, Dept., of Food). The entire scope of these two legislation is based on the minimum standard of Foods and related to prevention of food adulteration.

Therefore, PFA and FPO only deal with permitted ingredients, limits thereof and safety standards. Our food labelling standards and requirement are not very stringent and are governed by both these regulatory authorities as well as by Packaged Commodities Rules (PCR) under Weights and Measures Act. Both PCR and PFA have punitive power but FPO does not have. FPO can only cancel licences for any violations and default.

The food labelling standards are the minimum standards dealing with standards weights and measures of various categories of food, label size, size of the letters in the text of the declaration, nomenclature and other statutory declarations like maximum retail price etc. The product related information as required by law are minimal and limited to contains permitted colour and preservative, contains no fruit juice etc. The food laws in other countries even on these issues require that the manufacturers declare the name of food colour, preservative and other additives, if added.

The food products which are not classified under PFA Act are called proprietary products and for proprietary, designed and fabricated foods the ingredient list in descending order need to be declared in addition to other statutory declarations. If the manufacturer claims any nutritional or therapeutic property of the food, rules said that the label should indicate the quantity present. Thus if manufacturer claims in the label that it contains vitamin and minerals the limit or quantity present should be declared. But if it claims "minerals and vitamins added" there is no such requirement for declaring the quantity present, which can obviously misled the consumers.

The way processed foods, ready-to-serve food and fast food consumption are growing there is definitely a concern whether consumers are getting the adequate nutrition from their daily rations. Towards this end, nutrition labelling, if made compulsory, will be of great help. Firstly, there will be a basis of comparison of quality from the wide choice that is available. Secondly, the manufacturers will have to be more careful about the processing methods and standards that are adopted in order to preserve the wholesomeness of food because it will be the responsibility of the manufacturers to ensure conformance to declared standard till it is consumed.

We find in the market, lot of products including soft drinks, snacks, vegetable oil etc. with claim that the products are either low fat, fat free, low calorie, light (or lite) etc and these descriptions are used interchangeably. Consumers, in general, practically understand the same thing from all these claims and local food laws also don't differentiate them. Whereas US-FDA clearly defines such claims and manufacturers have to satisfy that. For example, as per US FDA low-fat means 3gm or less of fat per serving, fat free is 1/2 gm of fat per serving, and low calorie product should have 40 calories or less per serving. Light or lite is 50 percent less fat than standard product. US-FDA has also restricted the claims regarding relationships between a nutrient or food and the risk of a disease or health related condition. Only seven such relationships are allowed to be claimed.

They are—relationship between calcium and osteoporosis; fat and cancer, saturated fat and cholesterol and coronary heart disease, fruit and vegetables and cancer, sodium and hypertension, grain products and cancer, folic acid and neural tube defects. The food exporters to United States will thus have to conform to these requirements.

In India food labelling standard is still in its infancy and only provide very limited information towards product quality, safety and wholesomeness. Only recently a very select category of foods like baby foods and fruit and vegetable products have been taken up for deciding about the Environment Friendly Labelling Standards at the initiative of the Ministry of Environment and Forest.

5

Food Safety

The flow of food, which is the path that food follows from receiving through serving, is important for determining where potentially significant food safety hazards may occur. At each operational step in the flow, active management of food preparation and processes is an essential part of business operations. For instance, quick-service, full-service, and institutional providers are major types of food service operations. Each of these has its own individual food safety processes. These processes are likely to be different from a deli in a retail food store.

Some operations may have all three types of processes or variations of the three. Identifying the food process flows specific to your operation is an important part of providing a framework for developing a food safety management system.

Heating foods destroys bacteria, parasites, and viruses. But since this particular food flow does not include cooking, there is no step that will eliminate or kill bacteria, parasites, or viruses. An example is tuna salad that is prepared and served cold. Control in this process will focus on preventing:

— bacterial growth (e.g., storage under refrigeration),

- — contamination from employees (e.g., restriction of employees ill with diarrhea, proper handwashing, preventing bare hand contact with ready-to-eat foods, etc.),
- — cross-contamination from other foods (e.g., raw to ready-to-eat),
- — cross-contamination from soiled equipment (e.g., cleaning and sanitizing), and
- — obtaining foods from approved sources (e.g., a supplier of raw fish for sushi who adequately freezes fish to control parasites).

Food is prepared and served the same day. The food will be cooked and held hot until service, such as chili. Generally, the food will pass through the temperature danger zone only once before it is served to the customer, thus minimizing the opportunity for bacterial growth. The preparation step may involve several processes, including thawing a frozen food, mixing in other ingredients, or cutting or chopping. It is important to remember that added ingredients may introduce additional contaminants to the food. Cutting or chopping must be done carefully so that cross contamination from cutting boards, utensils, aprons, or hands does not occur. Control points at this operational step include good sanitation and handwashing.

During cooking, food will be subjected to hot temperatures that will kill most harmful bacteria, parasites, and viruses that might be introduced before cooking. It is the operational step where raw animal foods are made safe to eat, and therefore, time and temperature measurement is very important. Temperature of foods during hot holding must be maintained until service so that harmful bacteria do not survive and grow.

Failure to adequately control food product temperature is the one factor most commonly associated with foodborne illness. Foods prepared in large volumes or in advance for next day service usually follow an extended process flow. These foods are likely to pass through the temperature danger zone several times. The key in managing the operational steps within the process is to minimize the time foods are at unsafe temperatures.

In some cases, a variety of foods and ingredients that require extensive employee product preparation may be part of the process. A sound food safety management system will incorporate Standard Operating Procedures (SOPs) for personal hygiene and cross contamination prevention throughout the flow of the food. Before you set up a management system for your operational steps, there are several factors you should consider. Multiple step processes require proper equipment and facilities. Your equipment needs to be designed to handle the volume of food you plan to prepare. For example, if you use a process that requires the cooling of hot food, you must provide equipment that will adequately and efficiently lower the food temperature as quickly as possible. If you find that a recipe is too hard to safely prepare, you may want to consider purchasing pre-prepared items from a reputable source.

Developing Food Safety System

Although managers are responsible for designing the system, implementation involves the efforts and commitment of every employee. Education and training of both management and employees are important in their respective roles of producing safe foods.

In developing a food safety system, you need to identify the hazards that exist in the flow of foods in your operation from receiving to serving. Hazards include:

— pathogens or toxins present in food when you receive them,

— pathogens that may be introduced during preparation (example: using a raw animal food as one ingredient),

— pathogen growth or toxin production during storage, preparation, or holding.

— pathogens or toxins that survive heating, and

— contaminants, (i.e., pathogens, chemicals, physical objects), that are introduced to food by food workers or equipment. You need to identify the hazards associated with various foods and ingredients, such as:

— *Salmonella* and *Campylobacter jejuni* in raw poultry,

— *E. coli* O157:H7 in raw ground beef,

— *Staphylococcus aureus* toxin formation in cooked ham,

— *Bacillus cereus* spore survival and toxin formation in cooked rice,

— *Clostridium perfringens* spore survival and subsequent growth in cooked foods, and

— Hazards specific to seafood.

Ready-to-eat, potentially hazardous food is a special concern at receiving. Because this food will not be cooked before service, microbial growth could be considered a significant hazard for receiving refrigerated, ready-to-eat-foods. Having SOPs in place to control product temperature is generally adequate to control the hazards present at receiving of these products. Besides checking the product temperature, you will want to check the appearance, odor, color, and condition of the packaging.

Management of Storage

When food is in refrigerated storage, your management system should focus on preventing the growth of bacteria that may be present in the product. This is primarily achieved through temperature control. Special attention needs to be given to controlling and monitoring the temperatures of potentially hazardous ready-to-eat foods. When determining the *monitoring frequency* of product storage temperature, it is important to make sure that the interval between temperature checks is established to ensure that the hazard is being controlled and time is allowed for an appropriate corrective action.

For example, If you are storing potentially hazardous ready-to-eat foods under refrigeration, you may decide to set a critical limit for the refrigeration units to operate at 41°F or below. You may also want to set a target, or operating limit, of 40°F for example, in order to provide a safety cushion that allows you the opportunity to see a trend toward exceeding 41°F and to intervene with appropriate corrective actions.

Monitoring procedures for ready-to-eat food ideally include internal product temperature checks. You need to assess whether it is realistic and practical for you to do this, depending on the volume of food you are storing. You may choose to base your monitoring system on the air temperature of the refrigerated equipment as an SOP. How often you need to monitor the air temperature depends on:

— whether the air temperature of the refrigerator accurately reflects the internal product temperature -

(remember, your food safety refrigeration temperature must be based on the internal product temperature of the food stored within a refrigeration unit, not the air temperature),

— the capacity and use of your refrigeration equipment,

— the volume and type of food products stored in your cold storage units,

— the SOPs that support monitoring this process, and

— shift changes and other operational considerations.

Standard operating procedures can be developed to control some hazards and assist in implementing a food safety system that minimizes the potential for *bacterial growth* and contamination. The *control of cross contamination* can be done by separating raw foods from ready-to-eat products within your operation's refrigeration and storage facilities. Special consideration should be given to the storage of scombroid fish due to the potential formation of histamine, a chemical hazard.

Preparation of Food

Of all the operational steps in food processes, preparation has the greatest variety of activities that must be controlled, monitored, and in some cases documented. It is impossible to include in this model a summary guide that covers the diversity in menus, employee skills, and facility design that impact the preparation of food. The preparation step may involve several processes, including thawing a frozen food, mixing together several ingredients, cutting, chopping, slicing, or breading.

At the preparation step, SOPs can be developed to control some hazards and assist in implementation of a food safety system that minimizes the potential for *bacterial growth and contamination* from employees and equipment. Front-line employees will most likely have the greatest need to work with the food. A well designed *personal hygiene program* that has been communicated to all employees will minimize the potential for bacterial, parasitic, and viral contamination. Your program must include instructions to your employees as to when and how to *wash their hands.*

Procedures need to be in place that either *eliminate employees' hand contact with ready-to-eat foods,* or implement an alternative personal hygiene program that provides an equivalent level of control of bacterial, parasitic, and viral hazards. It is also very important to identify and *restrict ill employees* from working with food, especially if they have *diarrhea.*

Procedures must be in place to prevent cross contamination from utensils and equipment. Designated areas or procedures that separate the preparation of raw foods from ready-to-eat foods minimize the potential for bacterial contamination. Proper cleaning and sanitizing of equipment and work surfaces are an integral SOP to this operational step. Batch preparation is an important tool for controlling bacterial growth because limiting the amount of food prepared minimizes the time the food is kept at a temperature that allows growth. Planning your preparation ahead assists in minimizing the time food must be out of temperature at this operational step. Batch preparation also breaks the growth cycle of bacteria before they can reach dangerous levels.

When thawing frozen foods, maintaining proper product temperature and managing time are the primary controls for minimizing bacterial growth. Procedures need to be in place to minimize the potential for microbial, chemical, and physical contamination during thawing. Use of prechilled ingredients to prepare a cold product, such as tuna salad, will assist you in maintaining temperature control for this process.

Special consideration should be given to disallowing bare hand contact in the preparation of ready-to-eat foods. You need to control the introduction of hazards during preparation.

Management of Cooking

Cooking foods of animal origin is the most effective operational step in food processes for reducing and eliminating biological contamination. Hot temperatures will kill most harmful bacteria and with relatively few exceptions, such as cooking plant foods. It is at this step that food will be made safe to eat. Therefore, product temperature and time measurements are very important. If the appropriate product temperature for the required amount of time is not achieved, bacteria, parasites, or viruses may survive in the food.

Critical time and temperature limits vary according to the type of food. Employees should view ensuring proper cooking temperatures as an essential element in producing an acceptable product. A final cooking time and temperature chart for specific foods is included for your review. Simply reference the foods specific to your food establishment and incorporate the appropriate critical time and temperature limits into your management system.

You will need to determine the best system for you to use that will ensure that the proper cooking temperature and time are reached. Checking the internal product temperature is the most desirable monitoring method.

However, when large volumes of food are cooked, a temperature check of each individual item may not be practical. For instance, a quick service food service operation may cook several hundred hamburgers during lunch. If checking the temperature of each hamburger is not reasonable for you to do, then you need to routinely verify that the specific process and cooking equipment are capable of attaining a final internal product temperature at all locations in or on the cooking equipment.

Once a specific process has been shown to work for you, the frequency of record keeping may be reduced. In these instances, a record keeping system should be established to provide scheduled product temperature checks to ensure that the process is working. Special consideration should be given to time and temperature in the cooking of fish and other raw animal foods.

Cooling

One of the most labor intensive operational steps is *rapidly cooling* hot foods to control microbial growth. Excessive time for the cooling of potentially hazardous foods has been consistently identified as one of the factors contributing to foodborne illness. Foods that have been cooked and held at improper temperatures provide an excellent environment for the growth of disease causing microorganisms that may have survived the cooking process (spore-formers).

Recontamination of a cooked food item by poor employee practices or cross contamination from other food products, utensils and equipment is a concern at this operational step. Special consideration should be given to large food items, such as roasts, turkeys, thick soups, stews, chili, and large containers of rice or refried beans. These foods take a long time to cool because of their mass and volume. If the hot food container is tightly covered, the cooling rate will be further slowed down. By reducing the volume of the food in an individual container and leaving an opening for heat to escape by keeping the cover loose, the rate of cooling is dramatically increased.

Commercial refrigeration equipment is designed to hold cold food temperatures, not cool large masses of food. Some alternatives for cooling foods include:

— Using rapid chill refrigeration equipment designed to cool the food to acceptable temperatures quickly by using increased compressor capacity and high rates of air circulation;

— Avoiding the need to cool large masses by preparing smaller batches closer to periods of service;

— Stirring hot food while the food container is within an ice water bath; or

— Redesigning your recipe so that you prepare and cook a smaller or concentrated base and then add enough cold water or ice to make up the volume that you need. This may work for some water-based soups, for example.

Whatever the cooling method you choose, you need to verify that the process works. Once again if a specific process has been shown to work for you, the frequency of record keeping may be reduced. A record keeping system should be established to provide scheduled product temperatures checks to ensure the process is working.

Reheating

If food is held at improper temperatures for enough time, pathogens have the opportunity to multiply to dangerous numbers. Proper reheating provides an important control for eliminating these organisms. It is especially effective *in reducing contamination from bacterial spore-formers which survived the cooking process* and may have multiplied because foods were held at improper temperatures.

Although proper reheating will kill most organisms of concern, it will not eliminate toxins, such as that produced by *Staphylococcus aureus*. If microbial controls and SOPs at previous operational steps have not been followed correctly and Staph toxin has been formed in the food, reheating will not make the food safe. Incorporating a comprehensive personal hygiene program throughout the process will minimize the risk from Staph toxin. Along with personal hygiene, preventing cross contamination through the use of cleaned and sanitized equipment and utensils is an important control measure. *Special consideration* should be given to the time and temperature in the reheating of cooked foods.

Holding

There are three processes may involve holding. Proper temperature of the food while being held is essential in controlling the growth of harmful bacteria. Cold temperature holding may occur in Processes 1, 2, or 3. When food is held, cooled, and reheated in a food establishment there is an increased risk from contamination caused by personnel, equipment, procedures, or other factors. Harmful bacteria that are introduced into a product that is not held at proper temperature have the opportunity to multiply to large numbers in a short period of time. Once again management of personal hygiene and the prevention of cross contamination impact the safety of the food at this operational step.

Keeping food products at 140°F or above during hot holding and keeping food products at or below 41°F is effective in preventing microbial growth. As an alternative to temperature control, the Food Code details actions when time alone is used as a control, including a comprehensive monitoring and food marking system to ensure food safety.

Monitoring frequency may mean the difference between reheating the food to 165°F or discarding it. When determining the monitoring frequency of cold product temperatures, it is important to make sure that the interval between temperature checks is established to ensure that the hazard is being controlled and time is allowed for an appropriate corrective action. For example, If you are holding potentially hazardous ready-to-eat foods under refrigeration, such as potato salad at a salad bar, you may decide to set a critical limit at 41° F or below. You may also want to set a target, or operating limit, of 40° F for example, in order to provide a safety cushion that allows you the opportunity to see a trend toward exceeding 41°F and to intervene with appropriate corrective actions. Special consideration should be given to the time and temperature in the hot or cold holding of potentially hazardous foods to control pathogens.

Set-up and Packing

Set up and packing is an operational step used by some retail food establishments including caterers (e.g., restaurant/caterer or interstate conveyance caterer), commissaries, grocery stores (for display cases), schools, nursing homes, hospitals, or services such as delivery of meals to home-bound persons. Set up and packing can be controlled through an SOP and may involve wrapping food items, assembling these items onto trays, and packing them into a transportation carrier or placing them in a display case.

An example would be an airline flight kitchen where food entrees are wrapped, assembled, and placed into portable food carts which are taken to a final holding cooler. Hospital kitchens would be another example where patient trays are assembled and placed into carriers for transportation to nursing stations. Food may be placed into bulk containers for transportation to another site where it is served.

This operational step might not be considered a CCP, but it is a special consideration when setting up your program. This process can be controlled by strict adherence to SOPs to minimize the potential for bacterial contamination and growth, to eliminate bare hand contact with ready-to-eat foods, to ensure proper handwashing, and to ensure food comes into contact with cleaned and sanitized surfaces.

Following final assembly into either individual trays or into bulk containers, the food may be held for immediate service or for transportation to another site for service. This hot holding or cold holding operational step needs to be evaluated in the same manner as other holding operational steps on the worksheet. Temperature control or using time as a control measure during transportation, and holding and serving at a remote site must be evaluated and managed as part of your food safety system.

Serving

This is the final operational step before the food reaches the customer. When employees work with food and food-contact surfaces, they can easily spread bacteria, parasites, and viruses and contaminate these items. Managing employees' personal hygienic practices is important to controlling these hazards. A management program for employee personal hygiene includes proper handwashing, the appropriate use of gloves and dispensing utensils, and controlling bare hand contact with ready-to-eat foods.

Minimizing the growth of bacteria is also a concern at hot and cold holding customer display areas. Maintaining food products at proper temperature within these display units will control the growth of microorganisms. Special consideration needs to be given to minimizing contamination from the customer. Customer self-service displays, such as salad bars, require specific procedures to protect the food from contamination. Some suggestions for protecting food on display include:

— The use of packaging,

— Counter, service line, or salad bar food guards,

— Display cases,

— Suitable utensils or effective dispensing methods,

— Not mixing an old product with fresh, and

— Having employees monitor self-serve stations.

Preventing cross contamination from soiled utensils and equipment will minimize the potential for bacterial contamination of ready-to-eat foods.

Monitoring is observing or measuring specific operational steps in the food process to determine if your critical limits are being met. This activity is essential in making sure your critical food processes are under control. It will identify where a loss of control occurs or if there is a trend toward a loss of control of a critical food process.

Individuals chosen to be responsible for a monitoring activity may be a manager, line-supervisor, or a designated employee. Your monitoring system will only be effective if employees are given the knowledge, skills, and responsibility for serving safe food. Once your food safety system is implemented, you will need to confirm that it is effective over time. You may benefit from both internal (quality control) verifications and external verifications that may involve assistance from the regulatory authority or consultants.

Food Code Interventions

The provisions of the Food Code provide a foundation on which to develop a food safety system . Major interventions in the Food Code are demonstration of knowledge by the person-in-charge, employee health, no bare hand contact with ready-to-eat food, time and temperature control, and the use of a consumer advisory regarding the consumption of raw or undercooked animal foods. These interventions need to be addressed within the overall food safety program which may entail inclusion in SOPs.

Many provisions of the Food Code address the design of food establishments and equipment as well as acceptable operational practices. Adherence to design criteria and development of SOPs affect the food preparation environment. SOPs specify practices to address general hygiene and measures to prevent food from becoming contaminated due to various aspects of the food environment.

SOPs specific to your operation describe the activities necessary to complete tasks that accomplish compliance with the Food Code, are documented as a written reference, and are used to train the staff who are responsible for the tasks. Three purposes for establishing SOPs for your operation are to protect your products from contamination from microbial, chemical, and physical hazards; to control microbial growth that can result from temperature abuse; and to ensure procedures are in place for maintaining equipment.

SOP procedures ensure that:

— product is purchased from approved suppliers/ sources,

— the water in contact with food and food-contact surfaces and used in the manufacture of ice is potable,

— food-contact surfaces, including utensils are cleaned, saniti zed, and maintained in good condition,

— uncleaned and nonsanitized surfaces of equipment and utensils do not contact raw or cooked ready-to-eat food,

— raw animal foods do not contaminate raw or cooked ready-to-eat food,

— toilet facilities are accessible and maintained,

— handwashing facilities are located in food preparation, food dispensing, warewashing areas, and immediately adjacent to toilet rooms and are equipped with hand cleaning preparations and single-service towels or acceptable hand drying devices,

— an effective pest control system is in place,

— toxic compounds are properly labeled, stored, and safely used ,

— contaminants such as condensate, lubricants, pesticides, cleaning compounds, sanitizing agents, and additional toxic materials do not contact food, food packaging material, and food-contact surfaces, and

— food, food packaging materials, and food-contact surfaces do not come in contact with, and are not contaminated by physical hazards such as broken glass from light fixtures, jewelry, etc.

Procedures must be in place to ensure that proper personnel health and hygienic practices are implemented including:

— restricting or excluding workers with certain symptoms such as, vomiting or diarrhea,

— practicing effective handwashing,

— restricting eating, smoking, and drinking in food preparation areas,

— using hair restraints,

— wearing clean clothing, and

— restricting the wearing of jewelry.

FOOD SAFETY IMPLEMENTATION

Food safety, for our purposes, will refer to the handling of food and food contact items in a manner that reduces the risk of a foodborne illness outbreak. Food safety buzz is everywhere. It is a regular story for local news programs throughout the country. Equal attention is being given to the topic by foodservice equipment and supplies manufacturers, as they are eager to develop tools to assist with the implementation of safe food handling practices. Likewise, local health department inspectors and industry associations who promote food safety education are making sure that the topic's importance is clearly conveyed.

The intentions of all parties involved in the promotion of food safety are genuine. Implementation of safe food handling practices to this point, however, has been confusing and discouraging. The enforcement of food safety related requirements has been inconsistent. In addition, new food safety related requirements are rarely communicated clearly and expectations are rarely addressed with end users.

Another reason that the implementation of safe food handling practices has been difficult is (drum role please) ... money. It seems as though several members of the hospitality industry have focused on the potential profit from food safety related efforts first, and the benefits of food safety implementation second. As a result, progress has been slow.

Steps should be Taken

Implementing food safety principles makes good business sense. Sure, there may be some costs involved ... but look at the alternatives. What is the cost of a foodborne illness outbreak? Or, how about losing the stigma that food safety is a hush-hush topic and advertising your efforts to your customers. Let them know you are working your tail off to provide safe food. They will appreciate it.

Most food becomes "unsafe" through cross-contamination, the contact of food or food contact surfaces that are sanitary with those that possess organisms. The best way to prevent cross-contamination is proper receiving ... never let the contaminated product enter your facility. This is your first and best line of defense. To assist with this effort, a proper receiving area should be designed and included in every foodservice facility, regardless of size.

Should contaminated product slip through the back door, certain key design elements can help reduce the risk of cross contamination. First, be sure that your facility's design follows the flow of the food through the facility. In other words, limit or eliminate the possibility that potentially hazardous and ready-to-eat products will cross paths. By preventing the crossing of flow patterns in the kitchen, the risk of cross contamination is reduced.

Next, provide separate food preparation areas for potentially hazardous and non-hazardous foods, and separate these areas with physical barriers. For instance, provide separate vegetable and meat/fish/poultry preparation areas with a physical element between them. It is awful tough for chicken juice splatter to go through a wall and come in contact with ready-to-eat vegetables. Wallah ... cross contamination is prevented. The same principles of separation apply to the ware washing section of the kitchen, an area prone to cross contamination. Given the quantity of soiled and clean product in one confined area, separation is critical in ware washing.

Specific equipment may also be provided within a foodservice facility to assist with safe food handling practices. Such equipment selections include hands-free hand sinks and blast chillers, amongst many others. Hand sinks operated by electronic eye, foot lever, or knee valve activation reduce cross contamination that can occur from touching the faucet handles. The blast chiller is designed to reduce the internal temperature of a product to a safe temperature (below 41°F) in a time period that complies with food safety standards. Even if the unit is not purchased right away, providing the utility requirements during renovation or construction can save a great deal of money and provide valuable benefits down the road. Proper storage, whether of food or pots, pans, and utensils, is importnt as well.

Inspecting Incoming Food Materials

Note outside condition of carrier

The outside condition of the carrier may indicate contents were exposed to contamination while in transit.

Reasons:

1. Mud, dirt, water, oil stains or heavy insect debris on outside of carrier may have found its way to the products. For example, if the outside is wet, seepage may have occurred and contaminated the contents.
2. The shipment is more likely to be contaminated if the carrier is (1) an open-bed truck that is not properly covered; or (2) a truck or boxcar that is visibly damaged.

If doors of vehicle compartments have a seal, note if it is broken

The manufacturer affixed the seal to assure that you receive the high quality products he manufactured and shipped; if the seal is broken the acceptability of the products in the shipment should be suspect.

Reasons

1. A broken seal may indicate that some of the merchandise was stolen or that poor quality products

may have been substituted after your shipment was loaded and before arrival at your plant.

2. Toxic non-food items may have been added to the load, possibly contaminating your products, and removed before delivery of your shipment.

3. Compartment doors may have been opened to air-out foul odors shortly before arrival at your receiving dock. (Odors may have accumulated from trash, filth or spillage from previous shipment or your present shipment.)

Break Seal and open doors — at the same time note odor and temperature

Check for off odors, and high temperatures. If you find off odors in any shipment, or the temperature is high in refrigerated loads, it may mean the delivered products are unsafe.

Reasons

1. Foul odors may have been caused by the failure to remove food particles, filth and infestation resulting from previous shipments and to clean the carrier properly before loading your shipment.

2. The products may have been decomposed before being loaded, causing the off-odor.

3. The products may have absorbed harmful off-odors before shipment.

4. Toxic solvents, petroleum products or chemicals may have been carried with your shipment and unloaded before arrival at your receiving dock.

5. Frozen products, in the refrigerated load, may have been allowed to thaw during shipment, permitting the bacteria to grow and produce off-odors which accumulated.

6. High temperature, in refrigerated compartments, will allow the few bacteria normally present in the products to increase to dangerous numbers and to produce harmful decomposition products and odors.

Note condition of stacked cartons or other containers

Packages, cartons and similar type containers protect the products they contain. If they are broken, crushed or otherwise damaged, their contents will be exposed to possible contamination.

Reasons:

1. It is difficult to prevent contamination of food products in damaged packages, cartons or other containers.

2. Broken packages or containers may mean the product was contaminated and violative *before* it was loaded and shipped. The damage may have occurred while the product was in storage and contents exposed to insects, rodents or other contamination while awaiting shipment.

3. Harmful chemicals or pesticides may have entered the broken containers.

4. The shipment may have been improperly stacked or mishandled while loading or not protected while enroute your plant.

Look for evidence of insect, rodent and bird activity

Finding the presence of insects, rodent excreta, bird feathers or droppings or rodent urine is evidence products were exposed to contamination making them unfit for food.

Reasons:

1. Insects, rodents and birds are often carriers of disease-producing bacteria and parasites. Rodent excreta or droppings and urine can transfer these organisms to food products.

2. Products may have been contaminated with this filth before being shipped to your plant.

3. FDA will seize products stored in your warehouse if they are exposed to or contain insect or rodent or other filth. The filth does not have to be found in exposed products to make the product subject to legal actions.

Remove random samples of food containers for product examination

Random samples should be collected from the shipment and examined for contamination either on-the-spot or in the laboratory.

Reasons:

1. It is not possible and not practical to examine the contents of every packaged product in the shipment because the package is not saleable after opening and may become contaminated before being used.

2. Random samples that are representative of those in the entire shipment can be relied upon to show if products are acceptable or contaminated.

3. We can get a true picture of the entire lot *Only* if the samples are collected *Randomly* (that is, every 10th, 12th, 30th, or whatever, depending on the number in the shipment).

While unloading, note if non-food items are also in the shipment

Write in your report any non-food products (liquid or dry) that you find in the shipment with the food items.

Reasons:

1. Such products may be poisonous and can be a source of food product contamination. For example: there is no way you can be sure containers of non-food products will *NOT LEAK OR BREAK* during shipment or storage and contaminate the food items, making them POISONOUS OR OTHERWISE UNFIT TO EAT — which can happen without your knowing it since NO CHANGE IN THE LOOKS OF THE FOOD PRODUCTS MAY TAKE PLACE.
2. YOU DON'T HAVE TO FIND THE POISONOUS STUFF IN THE MATERIAL TO REJECT THE SHIPMENT. The Food, Drug and Cosmetic Act, which protect consumers, says in simple words that a food product is illegal if it is prepared, packed or held (or shipped) under conditions *which may have caused it to become contaminated* with filth or *which may have caused it to become dangerous to the health of consumers* (such as by exposing it to poisonous substances.

After unloading, observe inside condition of carrier

Floors and walls in disrepair and residue wastes from non-food shipments can cause contamination.

Reasons:

1. Cracks and broken boards are good hiding places for insects which could invade the shipment while in transit.
2. Residues from non-food items previously shipped in the carrier can contaminate food products.
3. Presence of cracks, splinters or broken boards may have prevented satisfactory cleaning and sanitizing of the carrier's interior, prior to loading your shipment, increasing the chance for contamination.

Preventing Foodborne Illness

More than 250 diseases can be caused by contaminated food or drink. Most are caused by bacteria such as Salmonella or Campylobacter. These bacteria most commonly are found in raw or undercooked foods of animal origin such as meat, milk, eggs, fish or shellfish. Most foodborne disease can be prevented by thinking twice - and following some simple food handling rules. This applies to people cooking at home and food service workers.

Consequences of foodborne illness range from mild stomach upset to flu-like symptoms, including nausea, vomiting and diarrhea, to severe symptoms such as kidney failure or death. Handwashing is the single most important means of preventing the spread of infection. Hand-transmission is a critical factor in the spread of bacteria, pathogens, and viruses that cause foodborne illness. In many cases, restaurant outbreaks have been traced to a single employee who failed to wash. "Parents can help prevent foodborne illness at home by washing their hands before and after they prepare food, and especially after handling raw meats, poultry or seafood, to prevent cross-contamination with other foods.

Cutting boards, knives and utensils must be kept clean and washed between uses. Foodborne illnesses related to food workers failing to wash their hands, or lack of properly working sinks, towels or soap, was a factor in 32 percent of the outbreaks. Cross contamination was a factor in 28 percent of outbreaks and ill or infected workers were identified in 13 percent.

Proper handling, cooking, storing, and serving of food can also prevent foodborne illness and contamination of the food, and keep naturally-occurring bacteria from multiplying. A basic rule is "keep hot food hot and cold food cold."

Each year, more than 30 million estimated cases of food poisoning occur in the United States alone. Foodborne illness kills an estimated 9,000 people each year nationally. The annual cost of foodborne illness in terms of pain and suffering, reduced productivity, and medical costs is estimated to be between $10 and $83 billion. Department of Health offers the following recommendations to prevent foodborne illness:

Purchasing food

— Shop for meats, including poultry and seafood, last.

— Keep raw meats separate from other foods, especially produce, in your shopping cart or grocery bags. Put meat in plastic bags to prevent drips that may contaminate other food.

— Do not leave meat or dairy products on the counter or in the car after shopping. Put foods into the refrigerator as soon as possible. - Wash your hands after handling raw meat in the store or at home. Raw meats that are wrapped for display often leak.

Preparing food

— Always wash hands before you begin to prepare food, and after handling raw meat, poultry or seafood. Use warm water, soap and paper towels. Antibacterial soap is a good idea.

— Keep your kitchen, utensils and dishes clean. Sanitize cutting boards, knives, or utensils that come into contact with raw meat by using a solution of bleach water (1 TBS/gallon).

— Sanitize countertops with antibacterial cleaner.

— Do not re-use wash cloths after wiping countertops, especially after cleaning up raw meat juice. - Serve food on clean plates. Do not use the same dish before and after you cook meat.

— Wash fruits and vegetables under running water.

— Re-heat leftovers to 165 degrees F.

— When cooking stuffed meats, ensure that it is heated to 165 degrees F even at the center.

—U se a food thermometer to make sure food is cooked to proper temperatures. All chicken and other poultry should be cooked to a minimum of 165 degrees F. Fresh roast beef is cooked to at least 130 degrees F. for medium rare. Ground beef should be cooked to 155 degrees F. Pork, including ham, should be heated to 150 degrees F. Other beef (steaks, roasts) and seafood should be heated to 140 degrees F. However, medium rare roast beef can be cooked safely to 130 degrees F.

Serving food

— At home, do not allow perishable food to sit at room temperature for more than two hours. Keep track of how long food sits on the table or the counter. After two hours, refrigerate it, reheat it or throw it away.

— When serving a large group, arrange and serve food on several small platters instead of one large one. Keep the rest of the food hot in the oven (set at 200-250 degrees F.) or cold in the refrigerator until needed.

— Hot foods should be kept at 140 degrees F. or warmer. On a buffet table, keep hot foods hot with chafing dishes, crock pots and warming trays.

— Cold foods should be kept at 45 degrees or colder. On a buffet table, keep cold foods cold by nesting dishes in bowls of ice.

Storing food

— Do not allow leftovers to cool at room temperature for more than 30 minutes. Then, promptly refrigerate.

— Keep leftovers in shallow containers (food depth less than two inches) so they cool quickly.

— Do not cover foods in the refrigerator until they have cooled down. Lids trap heat, creating more opportunity for bacteria to grow.

6

Organisational and Workforce Challenges

There are several strategic issues that will serve to influence the nature of the relationship between the hospitality firm and those individuals it employs to meet the needs of the customer of tomorrow. At the most macro level of understanding is the growing complexity of the transactions between people, institutions and people and businesses. This complexity results from the ever-increasing amounts of information that is generated, distributed and shared throughout society in general. It is almost overwhelming. The individual now has the choice regarding how much information they want to obtain about any subject and they are increasingly seeking to maximize their needs in this regard.

In the case of organization and employee relations this will result in more complex interaction and individualized relationships throughout the workplace. Most challenging of all will be the growing expectations and complexity in the transaction between guest contact employee and the customer. This complexity will necessarily result in new demands for better leadership across all levels of responsibility within the organization. This will also be driven in correlation with another macro force, the new worker.

The workforce of tomorrow will reflect the broad-based changes occurring in education which are taking place across the world. A shift from teacher centered learning to student centered learning is resulting in workforce entrants who are more independent in mind and spirit, who take responsibility for their own learning and are plugged into a cyber-based knowledge work. They are less likely to emerge from this environment being interested in jobs that do not challenge their intellectual capacity. Leading this new workforce will require new approaches to understanding and developing leadership skills.

This new worker will participate in a continuing shift in cultural imperatives emerging from what is frequently being referred to as the dot com generation, a euphemism for those who are developing their views and values from the internet. They will no doubt embrace such concepts as life long learning, greater matching of career and personal values and the desire for personal development. Developing within this generation are growing expectations for equality by all races and genders while at the same time witnessing an apparent contradiction in the growing intolerance for these differences. This will no doubt create a more complex work environment for both leader and follower.

A third issue affecting the management of human resources is a growing shortage of qualified labour to meet the increased complexity within all guest transactions. In the developed world, in the context of the current economic prosperity, unemployment is at its lowest in decades. With a growing demand for workers in the knowledge industry and the attractive working conditions it offers, few skilled workers are interested in working in basic service level occupations such as those available within the hospitality industry. Additionally, the demographics in the West are such that the age group that has met many of the industry's labour force needs is shrinking compared to other groupings.

In the developing world, the workforce is threatened due to the spread of disease; specifically those related to immune suppressed disorders like AIDS. In parts of southern Africa, it is not uncommon to lose as much as 10% of a firm's labour force as a result of this problem. These factors will no doubt compound the industry's already current struggles to obtain skilled employees. In addition to the labour shortage resulting from a shrinking youthful labour supply, it is also strained by the growing number of the so-called "baby boomer" group who will be retiring in the near future.

As the older worker transitions out of the labour force they will also have different job expectations that will change reward and compensation systems. Their work related goals may often be as much social as economic. They also will seek work-scheduling alternatives towards a shorter more flexible workweek. The *changing workplace* represents the fourth issue affecting the human resource function. The workplace is changing as a result of influences from the above forces.

The major change here is the flattening of the organization structure as the individual who has transitioned from a learner-centered environment as a student now expects the workplace to resemble this more individualized setting. In this context the organization must focus on setting standards and defining expected competencies.

The *global capital market system* is imposing demands for greater focus on adding value throughout the organization. Simply put, managers are expected to direct their attention toward producing products and services that will add value to the firm going forward. The attention must be on industry leading efforts to capture the customer of tomorrow and hold on to current ones. This not mean abandoning the romantic side of management often interpreted as good food and service, the high touch element of the hospitality business. It simply means that the hospitality enterprises must be thought of as businesses that are required to perform in competitive markets and produce financial gains that reward investors with returns in excess of their opportunity costs. This is not an easy task in today's environment.

Technology will alter the landscape in many ways. In particular, the change in the way customers look at the price value relationship will occur due to the increased transparency brought about by the Internet and electronic commerce. In particular, the growth of on-line auctions will force prices to remain highly competitive, almost to the point of commoditizing the industry. This then will focus the customer's attention on what products and services do they really value and what are they willing to pay for them.

In addition to these demand side issues, technology will change the internal management of human resources. From on-line sourcing of new employees to job change announcements within the firm, management information systems in support of the human resource function will change current practices. These macro forces have resulted in many micro forces that will create many challenges for human resource managers in next millennium. What is clear is that many shifts must take place in how the function of human resources management is practiced in this dramatically changing environment.

Changing Management Practices

The changes begin at the level of general management. The general manager must balance the traditional, internally focused view with one that incorporates an external, future oriented view. Managers must be able to anticipate change, invest in products and services that are future oriented and understand that these investments must produce returns in excess of the investor's cost of capital. The balance between craft and business skills has never been more important. This balance will set the stage for how the human resource function will be carried out. This ability to balance the art of hospitality with the demands for investment returns will alter the career paths of many in the industry today.

The traditional route through the functional areas of hospitality enterprises will not insure the top jobs. Expectations about career progress will have to shift from insuring great service to insuring great returns along with great service. The emphasis will be on owner relationships as well as on customer relationships. This will include a greater importance on managing the contract relationships with investors. Success will be based on competencies that will insure performance in this area of owner/investor relations.

Managing change and transmitting a value adding emphasis to all employees will become two of the most important of the competencies of tomorrow's manager. This will require greater creativity and vision on the part of managers with a focus on the future and the uncertainties presented by it. With the emphasis on adding value being driven by investors it is likely that there will be continued pressure to restructure the organization and do a way with many middle level management positions as responsibility is continually being pushed further down the organizational hierarchy. Those middle management positions that remain will shift orientation from task management to knowledge management, as greater attention will be placed upon the superior management of customer relationships and enhancing products and services.

Empowerment is being driven as much by this fact as it is by human resource professionals who advocate its use to improve leadership and motivation. A shift will occur in the way management looks at the resource provided by employees. They will be considered as less of a cost and more of an asset. Management will have to invest in that asset like it does in all its fixed versions. This includes the idea of significant investment in the development of that asset without the long held view that if this is done, that employee will leave and go someplace else and that investment will be used by the competition. This rather native and incorrect view will be unacceptable to tomorrow's employee who will make an employment decision more often on what the firm can do for them, with their own development being probably the most important consideration.

Performance evaluation and compensation systems will reflect the competency-based approach. Employees will expect to receive assistance in developing competencies and once they are successful, they will expect to be paid for this accomplishment. In fact, they will expect compensation even if the organization is unable to put those competencies to work immediately. The point here is that the employee of tomorrow will expect and seek development and personal growth opportunities and will not be willing to defer their rewards to some later time. Failure to manage this process successfully will result in difficulty retaining the new worker.

Leadership will change also. No more command control structures, participation will be essential. The manager of tomorrow will have to become a coach employing a learning organization model to solving the routine and exceptional problems of the business. With greater delegation of service delivery to the employee, they will grow more powerful in the formula of the business and will be expecting to be treated as partners, not task implementers in solving all types of problems. All this serves to make the entire human resource function more transparent.

Outsourcing will continue to develop across all functions of management. Entire departments such as housekeeping, accounting, front office and food and beverage will be considered as possible candidates for outsourcing. Also, the entire labour pool in a hospitality enterprise is likely to be purchased from an outsourcing supplier. As this trend continues it will change the human resource management function and the responsibilities of both operations and staff management. In many cases the HR function will cease to exist as a function within the enterprise as the outsourcing firm will handle most of this activity.

The responsibility left will be for leadership and motivation. Management will now have to concentrate on managing the outsourcing relationship. These evolving trends will impact how managers are trained and developed and this will change the skill sets needed. This will force dramatic curricular changes in those institutions that focus on developing hospitality industry professionals. It will also change the role of the teacher. The current body of knowledge presently taught, and highly criticized by think tank participants, will also have to change if these learning institutions are to succeed at developing tomorrow's new manager.

Individualism is a pattern of behaviour on the increase, both from the customer and the employee. This can be expected to continue. This translates into a different set of conditions in the workplace environment. The idea that the workplace should framed in an "obedience culture" is no longer acceptable. Power is now expected to be diffused throughout what was once referred to as the organization's hierarchy. This also suggests conditions that favour flexibility in everything from pay and work schedules to pension plans. Customization is no longer just the privilege of the customer.

The new worker will expect greater self-development opportunities, desiring to improve and perfect their personal effectiveness. Not only will this allow them to improve their social skill set when interacting with customers but it will also be of obvious benefit when seeking greater responsibility within the firm or when seeking other employment. This will become a very important benefit sought at all levels by all employees.

In fact, the phrase often used by interviewers when considering a new hire "what can you do for the firm" will be replaced by the prospect asking, "what can the firm do for me"? In this case, especially in tight labour markets, the prospective employee is becoming more demanding and discriminating regarding their own development and this can be expected to magnify as time goes by.

The individuality translates into the concept of the "free agent", meaning that people will assess their personal skill and competency inventory and seek to market it to the firm that offers the best deal, including signing bonuses. This will be especially true for those workers who will possess special knowledge capabilities needed in this complex and changing world. They in turn will expect to bring their knowledge tools into a team-based environment, not one based upon a command and control style of leadership.

The form of compensation and recognition expected will reflect both the individuality and team member effectiveness. Employees will be expecting to be compensated on their ability to translate the broad vision of the firm into everyday transactions. They anticipate being consulted in many areas and expect that their views will be honoured. They will expect to be given all the tools necessary to accomplish their tasks and to be empowered to use them. They also expect to be trusted and viewed as a community of employees, helping the organization to achieve its goals.

Employees will no longer expect the firm to provide lifelong work. They however expect to develop themselves in order to maximize lifelong career capabilities. Thus, they will value life long learning and opportunities for career development. This will become increasingly difficult as firms downsize and eliminate middle management positions. Career development becomes more difficult in flattened organizations. Thus, they will seek to develop competencies that will allow lateral job change and interesting work. They will expect compensation for competencies developed. This set of expectations will require more coaching and personalized leadership skills by those in authority.

The balance between work and private life will grow more important at all levels of the organization. For an industry that has betrayed this need for centuries, it raises perhaps the most significant challenge. The new worker will expect a work environment that is safe and healthful. They can expect and will demand greater say in how this environment should be shaped, including the benefits associated with it. For example, they will expect health insurance coverage that is commensurate with the changes created by the work environment. They will also expect management to provide an environment that will be able to absorb work force participants who have contracted AIDS related diseases without putting other employees into perceived risk settings.

Values and ethics become more important in the new work environment. There is a growing expectation for a greater display of moral values and integrity, especially on the part of the employee with respect to management behaviour. These issues will revolve around the employment, leadership and social responsibilities of the firm. This includes compliance with laws and norms including fairness. Employees would like to experience confidence in their leadership regarding this important new workplace expectation.

A growing spirituality exists throughout the workplace. This does not necessarily mean that people are becoming more religious, it only implies that everyone is expecting a higher moral ground, especially from leaders. Simply put, in a complex world where many feel a great uneasiness with the uncertainty surrounding this complexity, many look for a moral compass to guide them. This need will change further the leadership styles expected in the near future. It will expand what is meant by leadership, broadening the expectations of today's hospitality manager.

Role of New Technologies

Technology will continue to reshape the relationships between the employee and supervisor, and the employee and customer. First, management information systems will continue to enhance the human resource function and allow greater transparency between the employee and the firm. It will assist the employee in finding better work and self-development opportunities.

Managing information and data will become part of the job of every employee in increasing numbers. From data warehouses, to customized guest services information, the transaction between employee and customer is getting more sophisticated because of technology. This raises important questions about the jobs of tomorrow. Such questions as: what qualifications will be needed to meet technological changes in all jobs, how will this affect recruiting, compensation and development, how will the balance between hi-tech and hi-touch be accomplished, what investments will be required, how will authority be diffused by technology, what competencies are required, how will retraining be handled for those who do not possess competencies, what new jobs will be created and how will they affect the organization's structure? - will continue to force new thinking about the relationships between employee, customer and firm.

As the continuing challenge of finding qualified staff continues, it can be expected that there will be increased looks toward technology to assist in alleviating this problem. This can be expected to evolve further in places where it is becoming increasingly difficult to obtain the necessary staff to meet heightened levels of service. What is left to be defined is what elements of the service delivery system will be enhanced or supplied completely by technology?

Communication will no doubt continue to be revolutionized by technology. This includes the exchanges in a business to business environment along with the customer-employee interaction. These exchanges will be more information rich resulting in a growing set of expectations for quality, integrity and responsiveness. It is probably in this realm that the impact of technology will be felt the greatest in the near term future.

Changes will occur in the processes related to education and training as well as the content of what is communicated. Technology will influence how knowledge is shared, the timing of the sharing and the location. As Web based, cyber universities continue to expand their offerings, the learner will be able to enhance their skills anytime, anywhere, and at any pace.

Education, like so many other things will become more customized. The purchaser of this knowledge will become more discriminating. No longer will they accept marginal teachers, dated information and stale learning opportunities. They will seek the best, both in terms of the teacher and the delivery. In this new education market place, the merely passable teacher will not be eliminated, s/he will simply be relegated to the role of assisting the best by doing such tasks as grading, preparing materials and managing the logistics of the learning experience. They will no longer be able to hold a centre stage position.

Training programs, while always necessary for basic skill development, will also focus on developing personal effectiveness capability. As the new worker is required to do more and handle more complex settings they will be expected to become more personally effective in managing customer transactions that will result in added value to both the firm and customer. They will also be expected to be more effective at handling relationships which are growing more diverse among both customer and employee. Such skills as anticipation of customer and management needs, self-management, and personal responsibility for quality and economic value adding will be part of the training associated with the new worker and new manager. Along with this theme will be more efforts in multi-tasking and multi-skill development as jobs grow more complicated because the customer transaction grows more complex.

Training will be necessary, on a continual basis, in technology as this powerful element of business life becomes more of a competitive method. Such capabilities as managing information, the synthesis of ideas, and adapting and managing change are just a few of the areas in which training will be necessary. Technology will also influence how training will be done. Today, hospitality firms are developing personal coaches managed totally by multimedia components to guide the employee through everything from making pizza to serving as a help desk for night auditors. In many cases, these smart agent coaches are linked directly to the employee via microphones, ear pieces and digital cameras and are on demand.

Today's youth will no doubt be more comfortable with this style of instruction as opposed to the stressed out training manager or supervisor who often forgets basic behavioural skills when instructing employees on how to perform their jobs. The entire education and training process will become more learner-centered. Everything from numeracy to literacy skills will be capable of being learned in this new environment. New forms of certification and validation will emerge as cyber learning and customized development programs grow more important. Will it challenge the traditional benchmarks such as university degrees and trades recognition remains to be seen.

However, there is no doubt that many changes are occurring that will alter the landscape of all forms of training and education. The industry will face its most significant challenge here in trying to bridge the gap between the contemporary employee and manager who was trained and/or educated in the old model and those who are experiencing the new learning environment. Not only has this environment changed but so too has the body of knowledge. Thus, industry associations, consulting and training firms, schools and colleges and corporate training programs will experience a powerful need to bring the body of knowledge, along with the current and collective intelligence of present day management, into the new paradigm of management thinking.

CHANGING LABOUR ENVIRONMENT

Labour laws continue to mature within countries and across regions. In the international labour organization, a leader in improving the working conditions of all employees continues to be a driving force. Social conscience and awareness are bringing about greater focus on working conditions, especially in settings often characterized as "sweat shops". Child labour laws, moral issues such as prostitution, and exploitation of "have-nots" will help to shape a global standard for managing human resources. It can be expected that national governments will continue to feel the pressure to improve the working conditions for all people.

As diversity continues to impact the work environment, it can also be expected that governments and special interest groups will drive the cause for greater awareness, fairness and tolerance. Training and education programs will grow in number as businesses try to grapple with this challenge. This will not be a simple task in the context of a growing level of nationalism and intolerance. Labour unions while still influenced by regional and local environments will find it necessary to adjust to the discipline that capital markets place on businesses. The rigidity of job descriptions, categories and pay systems will have to change if businesses and countries try to compete in the global market place. Today, jobs are being transformed and transplanted as firms try to compete. There will be better partnerships between management and labour.

Working conditions will in many ways be legislated if businesses do not provide for the safety and health of their employees. As people power grows, brought on by the rush of democracy and belief in the power of people to change things, it can be expected that businesses, and entire industries will to asked, and in some cases required by law, to improve the entire work experience. Businesses will be required to demonstrate a much higher level of social responsibility.

This will have to change if the industry expects to attract and maintain employees. It will have to redefine the work environment. As it currently finds it fashionable to try to understand and capitalize on the lifetime economic value the customer has to the firm, so too will it have to define the lifetime value the employee brings to the firm. It will have to direct as much energy at trying to maximize the value and care it gives to each.

This revolution in thought and approach to the management of human capital will be difficult and perhaps represent one of the most difficult challenges to an industry steeped in the romance of traditional hospitality service. The millions of current managers across the globe must not only be retooled, they must be reconceptualized. This will not happen in one or two day training programs. It will be a transition and transformation that will take many years to accomplish. The challenge now falls upon the shoulders of the captains of industry, government and education to bring this about. It is yet to be determined if they will take up the challenge.

HYGEIN PRACTICES OF EMPLOYEES

Human beings are involved at all stages of food chain i.e. production, harvesting, packaging, transportation, loading, unloading, handling, etc. They are source of contamination. Illnesses associated with foods are primarily those transmitted by the faecal-oral route. Although raw produce can serve as a source of a variety of foodborne organisms, such as viruses, bacteria, protozoa, fungi, and parasitic worms, yet one should be gravely concerned about the presence of pathogenic bacteria, such as E. coli 0157:H7.

Methods directed towards reducing food safety risks in food production, harvesting and distribution operations must start with good sanitation and hygiene practices. The application of a good sanitation and hygiene programme should focus on the employees, environment, facilities, and transportation of fresh foods.

Worker's health and hygiene play a critical role in the controls for minimising microbial contamination of food. Faecal-oral diseases are the primary microbiological concerns that have been associated with food. Workers during growing, harvesting, sorting, processing, and packing food can spread these diseases. Infected food

Industry workers/employees have been implicated as the source of several foodborne outbreaks of gastro-enteritis, involving salads, cold food items, and ice.

Proper handwashing minimizes the spread of pathogenic bacteria and other microbial hazards, limiting the potential for contamination of produce. Good hygienic practices by all personnel who are involved in the harvesting, packing, and distribution of food are essential in the control of microbial and other biological hazards. Any individual in the agricultural environment (farm, packing areas, and transportation chain) who contacts food or equipment used in contact with food in agricultural areas presents a potential contamination risk.

All personnel, including those indirectly involved in food operations (such as, pest control operators), must comply with established hygienic practices. Infectious diseases, ill health accompanied by diarrhoea, open lesions (including boils, sores, or infected wounds), and other ailments are a source of microbial contamination that could contaminate food, water supplies, and other workers. Some microbial pathogens that can be transmitted by food contaminated by infected individuals includes, but is not limited to, the following:

1. Salmonella species,
2. Shigella species,
3. Staphylococcus aureus,
4. Streptococcus pyrogenes,
5. E. coli,
6. Giardia lamblia,
7. Hepatitis A virus.

Symptoms associated with infections by these pathogens may include diarrhoea, fever, vomiting, jaundice, and sore throat with fever. An employee suffering from any of these symptoms presents an increased risk of transmitting foodborne illness. Unfortunately most of the food companies do not practice regular medical check-up of their employees to prevent such incidences. It is suggested that:

— Operators train employees to report to the person in charge any information about their health or activities as they relate to diseases that are transmissible through food. Because of the high infectivity (ability to invade and multiply) and virulence (ability to produce severe disease) of Salmonella typhi, Shigella species, E. coli 0157:H7, or hepatitis A virus, any worker diagnosed with an active case of illness caused by any of these pathogens should be restricted from work assignments that involves contact with food or produce handling equipment.

— The supervisor, or the person in charge, should consider ways to monitor the health of their employees and take steps to reduce the chance of foodborne illness. For example, disposable rubber or similar gloves, leak-proof band aids, or other corrective measures for minor cuts should be provided for use as necessary to the personnel who may have contact with produce.

— More importantly, the person in charge should ensure that workers with diarrheal disease are not working with food or any equipment used in the harvesting and processing of food.

— Workers should be taught to report symptoms caused by illness, infection, or other source that is associated with acute gastrointestinal illness such as: diarrhoea, fever, vomiting, jaundice, or sore throat with fever, a lesion containing pus such as a boil or infected wound that is open or draining and that is located on parts of the body that might have contact with food or produce harvesting and processing equipment.

Role and attitude of senior managers is very crucial. Many time senior managers ignore the need of training and re-training of employees. Such short-sighted managers are doing disservice to their companies because poor quality and unhygienic food is eroding their companies' good will in market place. All employees, including supervisors, full time, part time and seasonal personnel, should be trained in good hygienic practices. Computer can be used to train people either through animation films of video films.

Processors or growers may want to consider establishing a training programme that would include a system to monitor and evaluate compliance with established sanitary practices. The operators should also consider follow-up training sessions to encourage adherence to good hygienic practices. The biggest challenge is to change the mindset of employees and facilitate the learning of new techniques.

The focus of any training programme should include, but is not limited to, the following:

— The importance of good hygiene.

— All personnel should understand the impact of poor personal cleanliness and unsanitary practices on food safety.

— Smoking or eating in areas where food is present can contaminate the produce because of the potential that the hands and food-contact surfaces may become contaminated.

— Insanitary personal practices such as scratching the head, placing the fingers in or about the mouth or nose, and indiscriminate and uncovered sneezing or coughing may contaminate food or any handling equipment. Within packinghouses, hair can be a direct and indirect vehicle of contamination. Workers may contaminate their hands by touching their hair. For enclosed facilities, operators may want to consider the use of hair restraints to keep dislodged hair from ending up in food and to deter employees from touching their hair.

— Thorough handwashing after each absence from the workstation, after using the bathroom, before and after eating, and before commencing work is very important. Many of the diseases that are transmissible through food may be harboured in the employee's intestinal tract and shed in the faeces. Thorough washing of hands with soap and warm water helps to stop the spread of germs. Employees should be taught proper handwashing techniques, that include: hand washing with warm water (if available); proper use of soap; and thorough scrubbing (including cleaning under finger nails and between fingers), rinsing, and drying of the hands.

— The importance of using sanitation facilities. All employees should be encouraged to use on-site latrines and to avoid eliminating wastes outside of these facilities. The use of well maintained sanitation facilities for waste elimination helps reduce the potential for cross contaminating fields, produce, other workers, and water supplies, and increases the likelihood that employees will wash their hands after using such facilities.

— Employee must feel proud and help colleagues in achieving sanitation and hygienic standards.

In competitive business environment, good knowledgeable employees are the most important assets. You take care of them they will take care of your business interests. Careful inspection of the establishment, can help you to see if the operation could face quality as well as regulatory problems.

No one wants to deal with poor quality products. If your business gets bad reputation of poor quality, or otherwise negligent, your prospective customers will start looking for other better options if not at least cleaner suppliers. It makes good business sense to keep your operation healthy and reputable. Safe and quality products helps you to do this. The food laws and regulations that PFA authorities enforce apply to firms that receive or ship food in inter state trade. The requirement places the prime legal responsibility for safe and quality foods, adequately labelled, upon the food processor.

If you just store foods, you too are legally bound to prevent contamination of the food while it is in your possession either in factory or in trade. This is the law. In terms of cost and manpower, self inspection is the most reasonable means of helping to ensure a satisfactory food processing and storage operation, and a trouble free relations with authorities.

There are many problem areas, which if left unchecked, can become severe hindrances in your efforts to maintain a sanitary food operation free of compliance problems. First and foremost is the rodent (usually, rats and mice). This is the major problem area for export consignments. Rodents carry many diseases and parasites which, because of their biological similarity to people, can be transmitted to man. These diseases and parasites include leptospirosis, salmonellosis, tapeworms, trichinosis and others. Rodents will deposit excreta, urine and other filth on food products and around your production facilities. They will also gnaw on materials in order to build nests. Rodents contaminate much more than they eat. Against rodents, you cannot take the security of your plant or firm for granted. Some rodents can walk along telephone wires or leap horizontally 18 feet. They can squeeze through the gaps ,width of a pencil or drop 50 feet without being killed. Their instinct for survival is high, and they can deviate from "normal" behavior patterns to trick man. They are extremely prolific creatures, and once they've infiltrated into your operations, your problems will multiply.

Birds also carry diseases and parasites potentially hazardous to people. They are capable of flying through any open window, door or other gaps in your building, and, like rodents, will leave in sanitary droppings that can contaminate your plant and your food products. Insects seek heat, moisture and darkness, and if it is once in, can be even more elusive than rodents or birds. However, they aren't invisible - they leave trails in the dust, and it can also be spotted around likely insect hideouts: holes, damp places, behind boxes and in seams in bags and folds of paper.

Like rodents, some insects - notably cockroaches - have a highly developed survival instinct and they are adaptable - they can develop an immunity to poisons you use within a few insect generations. They are even more prolific than rodents. With their hairy legs, they spread dirt, debris and bacteria around your firm. They carry either within or outside of their bodies the causes for many serious diseases and ailments such as boils, food poisoning and typhoid fever. In dealing with any of the above pest problems, you may want to try to cope with them on your own, but it is highly recommended that you seek the help of a good pest control operator, or ,.exterminator." The results will probably be better, and in the long run, this may be a more cost effective method. if you were to take all the rodents and insects in the world, they would be outnumbered by the bacteria to be found in one vat of spoiled egg batter.

Bacteria are a worse problem than any of the previously mentioned creatures because they can't be seen, yet they can sicken or kill just the same. Bacteria cannot be eliminated, but they can be defeated. Like any creatures, bacteria need a combination of food, water and proper temperature to survive. By regulating the availability of each, you can take a big step toward keeping their population down.

Molds will grow on almost anything, especially where there is moisture. The presence of mold in a product is an indication that the product contains excessive decomposed material and may also indicate in sanitary practices on the part of the processor. Molds can make you ill, and scraping off mold or getting rid of the one "bad apple" doesn't always solve the problem.

While the other problem areas are active, aggressive opponents, chemical contaminants can only become a problem through misuse or neglect - yet the end result of their presence can be equally disastrous. Still, this is one of the easier problems to control.

This brings us to the most important and crucial problem area-ignorance and carelessness. As a problem, this can be just as dangerous as any of the proceeding, but it can be combated by applying the certain guidelines, and byjust using common sense. Now, let's get on with the tactics for waging an offensive against the problems.

Self-inspection

Self-inspection is a most cost effective way for you to maintain a firm that is in compliance with legal requirements for food processing and storage. By assuming the role of an investigator, you can uncover potential problems and solve them before they become big problems.

Good Manufacturing Practices

Cleaning Procedure

Food employees shall clean their hands and exposed portions of their arms with a cleaning compound in a lavatory by vigorously rubbing together the surfaces of their lathered hands and arms for at least 20 seconds and thoroughly rinsing with clean water.

Employees shall pay particular attention to the areas underneath the fingernails and between the fingers. Food employees shall clean their hands and exposed portions of their arms immediately before engaging in food preparation including working with exposed food, clean equipment and utensils, and unwrapped single-service and single-use articles and:

— After touching bare human body parts other than clean hands and clean exposed portions of arms;

— After using the toilet room;

— After caring for or handling support animals or aquatic animals.

— After coughing, sneezing, using a handkerchief or disposable tissue, using tobacco, eating, or drinking.

— After handling soiled equipment or utensils;

During food preparation, as often as necessary to remove soil and contamination and to prevent cross contamination when changing tasks; When switching between working with raw food and working with ready-to-eat food; and After engaging in other activities that contaminate the hands.

Where to Wash

Food employees shall clean their hands in a hand washing lavatory and may not clean their hands in a sink umd for food preparation, or in a service sink or a curbed cleaning facility used for the disposal of mop water and similar liquid waste.

A hand sanitizer and a chemical hand sanitizing solution used as a hand dip shall have active anti microbial ingredients that are recommended as safe and effective for application to human skin as an Antiseptic Hand wash

If a hand sanitizer or a chemical hand sanitizing solution used as a hand dip does not meet the criteria specified, after the use the contact surface i.e. hands should be thoroughly rinsed in clean water before hand contact with food or by the use of gloves; or limited to situations that involve no direct contact with food by the bare hands. A chemical hand sanitizing solution used as a hand- dip shall be maintained clean and at a strength equivalent to at least 100 mg/L chlorine. Food employees shall keep their fingernails trimmed, filed, and maintained so the edges and surfaces are cleanable and not rough.

Outer Clothing

Food employees shall wear clean outer clothing to prevent contamination of food, equipment, utensils, linens, and single-service. An employee shall eat, drink, or use any form of tobacco only in designated areas where the contamination of exposed food; clean equipment, utensils, and linens; unwrapped single-service and single-use articles; or other items needing protection can not result.

In case of urgency, a food employee may drink from a closed beverage container if the container is handled to prevent contamination of the employee's hands; the container; and exposed food; clean equipment, utensils, and linens; and unwrapped single-service and single-use

Food employees experiencing persistent sneezing, coughing, or a runny nose that causes discharges from the eyes, nose, or mouth may not work with exposed food; clean equipment, utensils, and linens; or unwrapped single-service or single-use articles.

Hair Restraints Effectiveness

Food employees shall wear hair restraints such as hats, hair coverings or nets, beard restraints, and clothing that covers body hair, that are designed and worn to effectively keep their hair from contacting exposed food; clean equipment, utensils, and linens; and unwrapped sin le-service and sin le-use articles.

Since ages food is an area of commercial interest to mankind. Food Safety was discussed in various ways in various societies. In India, Good Manufacturing Practices were integral part of our cultural and social practices and were designed to take care of basic food safety requirements. Recall your childhood, when mother used to order "wash your hands before touching any food product", keep unwashed utensils far away from kitchen, keep your shoes out of kitchen, etc. etc. These methods are effective and even valid in modern science age.

Traditionally, Indian Society is hygiene conscious. In recent years because of increased commercialisation and adoption of unhygienic habits for undue commercial gains and lack of resources available to the people in the food trade coupled with environmental pollution, food hygiene has become a major issue of concern in international trade.

Food safety has become a issue of great interest to everybody in food trade when the United States FSIS Pathogen Reduction/HACCP rule published in July 1996 combines the concepts of Hazard Analysis and Critical Control Point (HACCP) systems with the FSIS requirement for written Sanitation Standard Operating Procedures (SSOPs). However HACCP and SSOPs are only part of a total food safety system. Good Manufacturing Practices provide the foundation for SSOPs and HACCP. It is important to have a clear understanding of the relationship between the GMPs, SSOPs and HACCP plans for compliance of various food safety regulations.

GMPs' pre-requisite programmes comprise the basic, universal steps and procedures that control operating conditions within establishments and ensure favourable conditions for the production of safe food. These differ from HACCP systems which focus on the critical points in a manufacturing process that affects food safety. GMPs are the control factors that relate to the entire operation and are not process-specific. GMPs include programmes such as facilities/grounds, equipments/utensils, pest control, receiving and storage, process control, product recall and personnel training.

Prior to the development and implementation of HACCP plans, an establishment should first review existing programmes and verifies that all GMPs are in place and effective. Effective GMP programmes ensure that HACCP plans focus specifically on the critical control points (COPs) necessary for product safety. If any portion of the GMPs is not adequately controlled, there is possibility for a HACCP plan to be less effective in ensuring product safety.

Components of Good Manufacturing Practices (GMPs)

GMPs are like any policy programme any manufacturer has implemented. They require a written programme, an appropriate training programme and schedule, a maintenance schedule and most importantly management commitment. Management commitment is the vital component of any programme the company implements. Management's role takes on many forms from providing funds, guidance, human resources, to following the rules themselves.

Once management has committed to the implementation of a programme other components will fall in place. Without this no amount of investment or external assistance will deliver results.

Written Programme and Records

The written programme will serve as the base for other components. A good written programme includes who, that, where, when, why and how of the programme. It should clearly explain the scope of the programme, responsible individuals, its importance, parameters, monitoring activities and records, corrective actions and records and verification activities. A multi-disciplinary team made up of individuals with technical and operational expertise should write the programme. In small units, entrepreneurs may take help of external well-qualified food industry professionals or can go for training themselves.

The written programme should be written at a level that is appropriate for the educational level of employees and in a language they understand. Furthermore, it should clearly set forth an effective communication system i.e. the record keeping system and the expectations of the record keeping system. It is however an effort, which is required once, and later it will act as a basic guide and can be modified as and when required to upgrade the quality standards.

A record keeping system creates the environment in which employees communicate with one another. Its proper design and implementation directly effects how information is shared and problems are solved. The record keeping system must be a proactive vehicle of communication, desigred primarily to be useful. Monitoring and corrective action records should be designed not only with the monitor in mind, but also the auditor.

Records should include a brief description of parameters being monitored corrective actions to be taken by the monitor, product code/code date, date, time, findings, monitors initials and any other appropriate information. Records should be reviewed, prior to being filed, for accuracy and to ensure that all the parameters of the programme were met and appropriate corrective actions taken. Monitors should be carefully chosen and appropriately trained. They should have good written communication skills, to make the records that ensures the proper compliance.

Training Programme

Next to management commitment, an effective training programme and schedule are critical to the effectiveness of the GMP programmes. Without the proper training of all employees, the effectiveness of GMPs is jeopardised. Training of employees and of your own will help translate your dream into reality not only in terms of quality but also in terms of profits. Thus it is vital to develop human capital to face competition. There should be stress on the importance of both employee participation and employee accountability.

Literacy and language are two very important issues to be considered in developing the appropriate training programme for GMPs and other food safety programmes, because all persons involved in production processes may not be from the same place or may not be of the same educational evel. In addition, people learn visually and/or audibly, in other words, there are people who learn by reading or seeing, some learn by hearing and some learn by the combination of the both. An effective training programme will incorporate different deliveries of information.

Furthermore, an effective training programme is structured in such a way that the employees are told in advance what will be taught, and then they are trained and finally a review is done of what they have learnt. Once the programme has been developed, trainers must be selected and trained. Trainers should be chosen carefully and should be selected on the basis of his/her training skills and not by job description or position they hold in the company or department. It is a well acknowledged fact that a good player may not necessarily be a good coach always.

Training schedule development should take into account turnover rate, and should have update or reminder sessions as well. All new employees, regardless of job, should go through an initial training session. Many times companies prefer on the job training to save time or money but on the job training (OJT) is not an effective way to train employees for GMP or food safety programmes. OJT hampers the learning process of new concepts and new benchmarking.

In some situations it is conceivable to have "new employee" training on a daily basis. All training activities should be documented including who received the training, the date and the type of training given. This will help in later date to identify the training needs of the employees for further up-gradation.

Scientific Inputs for Programme Maintenance

In today's world scientific and commercial information undergo change very fast. Like facilities and equipment, written programmes need to be maintained to ensure their effectiveness. A maintenance schedule for written programmes should be based on changes in your facility environment or new scientific developments. Employee turnover, new process introductions and facility layout changes are just a few issues that could trigger a review of the written programme. In addition, any time you reassess food production and safety/programmes the GMPs should also be reassessed.

With few exceptions, governments have recognised the importance of liberalising agricultural markets. Countries have turned to the promotion of market-oriented economic activities carried out by the private sector from a situation of dominant state control. The process is, not complete and continued effort is required to ensure that government policy effectively incorporates and addresses issues of marketing liberalisation and helps to overcome the constraints faced by the private sector.

The private sector is now more or less universally acknowledged for its dynamism in carrying out marketing functions. In many countries, the so-called "informal" sector must be encouraged for its efficient use of limited resources vitality and adaptability, witnessed by the way it has responded to opportunities presented by the liberalisation of markets. "Quality product" in affordable price is the message for the companies to survive in market place.

One of the basic ingredients is mindset in ensuring food quality. Commonsense is widely applied in quality management in food industry. English dictionary defines common sense as conforming of practical wisdom and judgement or practical good sense gained by experience of life and not by special study. In practice, it is the art of making judgements and decisions or doing sound things with existing knowledge, and expected to exercise common sense regularly if proper job is to be done.

Common sense is not a sixth sense, intuition or extra-ordinary perception. Rather, it is an integration of all the knowledge a person possesses on a given subject at a given moment regardless of whether the knowledge is technical, scientific (pure or applied, supported by theory or is empirical) or based on personal experience. Furthermore, this knowledge does not always have to be specially related to the subject in question, provided some analogy can be firmly established between the subject to be analysed and some previous experience or knowledge.

The main ingredients in applying common sense are:

— *Observation*: Sharp observers tend to possess more common sense. As someone said, it is one thing to look, another thing to see and a different thing to rationalise what one sees.

— *Objectives and Knowledge*: Simple observation is not enough. One must have clear objectives and knowledge of clear objectives and knowledge of a given subject - the knowledge and experience accumulated by people in general and oneself in particular. Of course, it is not possible to know every thing, but the clear the objective and more knowledgeable one is the better.

— *Judgement*: Good judgement is a prerequisite of common sense. Comparing observation, objective and knowledge will give us a difference that must be judged and analysed. Priority should be given to things observed and their relative impact on the goal pursued assessed before issuing an effective statement and/or deciding on the next course of action. Obviously, judgement is the most difficult link in the chain which forms common sense, particularly when dealing with uncertainties, incomplete knowledge (not to mention ignorance) using analogies that are sometimes imperfect.

Common sense is not taught at school but studies can help, provided emphasis on the banking of knowledge, dogmatic attachment to fashionable theories or bewitchment with the beauty of figures do not preclude free and creative thinking. Common sense is also necessary when deciding what to test and the best way to do so. The tests should be quick, simple and relatively cheap. Technical and scientific knowledge has to be combined with common sense. There should be clear-cut distinction between quality and implication of the end use.

Awareness is only a part of what is involved. One should take into account quality targets, review the knowledge and experience available on the problem in question and then decide how to solve it. A basic criterion is opting for the most economical solution befitting prevailing information needs or action. Common sense implies a process of economic optimisation of the cost of achieving and sustaining a given quality. It certainly does not mean instant saving but rather savings in the long run and avoiding quality problems.

Generalisations are not necessarily a common sense exercise and if applied to specific problems are certainly harmful. Undoubtedly, rational thinking and evaluation should be used as much as possible when trying to solve a problem, but solutions chosen should be the most simple and viable. Common sense is necessary, especially in the absence of tangible scientific and technical knowledge. Common sense is essential for understanding and solving quality problems arising from different socio-cultural situations. However, the main application is probably to be found in bridging the knowledge of people trained in different subjects but involved in similar areas of work.

Common sense cannot be taught, but there are ways by which it can be enhanced:

— *Increasing Practical Knowledge*: This does not mean only studying books, journals or magazines but also making an effort to adopt existing knowledge to our conditions (especially in countries like India). Informal training such as visiting other factories to observe operations and routines can, in this case, be more useful than formal training. A planned visit to established factories which produces more or less the same type of product or facing same types of problems is an investment in common sense.

  Management should also be aware of what happens to the product from the time it leaves the factory to the time it is consumed / utilised to better understand the requirements and complaints of brokers and consumers alike.

Practical knowledge can also be increased through simple applied research carried out in factory. For example, Shelf-life studies by variable processing parameters in different conditions, Packaging material suitability for long distance transportation, etc.

— *Co-operative Effort*: To take full advantage of common sense in decision-making exercises, working, as a group is ideal. All good managers are aware of this but perhaps the Japanese idea of 'Quality Circles' whereby the experience and knowledge of everyone are drawn upon, is the best example of co-operative effort and also working very well in many Indian companies. It does not only mean a sharing of knowledge but also an increase in observation and judgement capabilities.

— *Efficient Use of Communication*: The interaction between research institutes or universities and industries is unsatisfactory in many countries, particularly in underdeveloped and developing countries, including India. Communication between these two is virtually non-existent. It must be changed if we want to transform theory into practical knowledge and apply it to production.

As in other cases, it would probably need a book to define the idea but what can be said is:

a) Industry should take the initiative, without looking for excuses for not adopting quality requirements, and

b) Industry should ask the questions and hope for right answers. It is due to lack of common sense that knowledge is left on the shelf. Very often emerging concepts are ignored not only by industry but also institutions. It is a lack of common sense that makes institutes concentrate on fashionable research subjects or remain idle while industries (or even producers at artisanal level) seek technical advice on simple matters. Finally, it does not make sense that industry, which helps the institutes, does not use their services because there is a serious gap and lack of trust between industry and institutions.

Chef Training

We can divide what you would probably classify as cooks into three distinct sub-groups, according to their potential. We call them: cooks, artists, and managers.

The first group, cooks, are simply that. These are people who are capable of following directions and providing skilled kitchen labour, but are either not motivated to, or capable of taking extra responsibility. I'm talking about the responsibility for creativity and the responsibility for leadership. These people are the backbone of every kitchen. It's not that they can't create, or lead for brief periods; it's just that they don't want the stress of doing it all the time. They do need to be challenged though - if you leave them doing something boring or repetitious for too long, they'll leave.

The second group are the artists. They are the true innovators, the ones who can create new flavours, textures, visual delights; assimilate new produce; and stimulate the senses. They are a small minority; We believe the ratio of truly talented artists to cooks is about 1:50. They are very valuable, but can be very difficult people - they don't think in a straight line using normal logic; that's where their creativity seems to come from. Many are tortured souls and some are temperamental tyrants; few are good leaders.

If you are operating a small restaurant at the top end of the market you often have no choice but to put an artist in charge as Chef. You probably need innovative food to justify your high pricing. We don't have a problem with this as long as you don't expect them to lead too many staff, and as long as you are prepared to manage them and ride shotgun over their wage and food costs. Don't expect them to do it; the true artist is not the least bit interested in your practical business problems, or in accepting responsibility or discipline.

To run a large kitchen brigade you need a manager. These are the leadership cooks, the practical souls who can handle people, words, numbers and commercial reality. They are not usually very creative - they're better plagiarises than innovators - but the better ones do run a tight ship and they do keep staff motivated and happy. They're quite rare as well; the same 1:50 ratio applies when you're searching for them.

Management Chefs often have delusions about their creative abilities and have to be taught to recognise their limitations. We've had great success structuring kitchens with a manager as Chef and a few artistic or semi-artistic cooks under them to supply the creativity. We seem to get good synergy once everyone recognises their strengths and weaknesses.

If you put an artistic Chef in charge of a large brigade you can have a recipe for disaster. They will tend to hog all the creative tasks for themselves and may stifle self expression on the part of the other cooks. They will often exhibit bizarre and inconsistent people handling skills, and may tend to let costs get out of control. Some seem to pride themselves on only using the most expensive ingredients and processing everything by the most labour intensive methods. Others get hysterical if a dish is returned by a waiter or a customer puts salt on their food.

It is important to carefully plan the structure of your kitchen to match the requirements of your business. Most kitchens don't need a true artist, all they need is a competent mimic. What most of them do need is a good manager. To put it another way, we believe that ninety percent of the industry needs competent food, produced cost-effectively.

Our current shortage of experienced cooking staff is creating the situation where young and inexperienced cooks are being pushed into supervisory positions before they have the skills or the experience to handle these roles. Rapid expansion of the industry has caused supply and demand problems, it has reached the point where it is now common for third and fourth year apprentices to be in charge of kitchen staff. This problem is made worse by business owners who deliberately try to save money by hiring apprentices to run their kitchens instead of fully qualified cooks.

On the surface, an opportunity for young people to progress at an early age may not seem such a bad thing but in reality the reverse can be true. The stress of becoming the meat in a triple sandwich between the owner, staff and customer has caused a disturbing number of young cooks to rethink their careers and leave the trade.

When you examine the training given to cooks during their apprenticeship there is a natural concentration on the technical skills of food preparation - after all, cooking is a craft trade. The problem is, when you take a person who has been educated to work in a creative way with inanimate objects and place them in charge of people who do not always behave predicably, open conflict and other forms of potentially destructive behaviour often result.

The progression from trade through supervision to management is really a second apprenticeship. A few lucky people are natural leaders; of the rest, a fair percentage have the capacity to learn to be a good leader and the remainder should never be put in charge of other people.

If you put a cook who has had no supervisory training in charge of others, there is a fair chance there will be difficulties with staff handling. This can be frustrating in the extreme, and lead to the point where stress is relieved in a destructive manner - the infamous tantrum being a notable example.

Effective leadership requires a number of skills on in addition to those present at the end of a technical apprenticeship period. Demonstration of performance in the basic cooking role does not automatically make the person ready for promotion. In fact, promotion often leads to the loss of a good cook and the gain of an ineffective Chef.

To learn appropriate leadership skills is not a terribly expensive or time consuming process; the education is available through outside training courses provided by independent training organisations, or some hospitality colleges. To become good at them is another matter; like any skills, practice makes perfect, and proficiency can take time.

The growth of the industry is opening up opportunities for a new breed of 'managing chefs' to continue on a career path which was not previously available. Unfortunately, many cooks will never be able to take advantage of these new positions - because they do not have the skills.

Bibliography

Breault, J. L., *Development and evaluation of a training manual on feeding children with special needs, birth through age five.* Kansas State University, Manhattan, 1995.

Carroll, P., Caplinger, K. J. , & France, G. L., "Guidelines for counseling parents of young children with food sensitivities", *Journal of the American Dietetic Association, 92*(5), 602-603, 1992

Conklin, M. T., Nettles, M. F., & Martin, J., "Modified meals: Strategies for managing nutrition services for children with special needs", *School Foodservice and Nutrition, 52*(7), 44-52, 1998

Cannella, P. C., Bowser, E. K., Guyer, L. K., Borum, P. R., "Feeding practices and nutrition recommendations for infants with cystic fibrosis", *Journal of the American Dietetic Association, 93*(3), 297-300.

Chumlea, S. C., Guo, S. S., & Steinbaugh, M. L., "Prediction of stature from knee height for black and white adults and children with application to mobility-impaired or handicapped persons", *Journal of the American Dietetic Association, 94*(12), 1385-1388, 1391, 1994

Gandy, L. T., Yadrick, M. K., Boudreaux, L. J., & Smith, E. R., (1991). Serving children with special health care needs: Nutrition services and employee training needs in the school lunch program, *Journal of the American Dietetic Association, 91*(12), 1585-1586.

Hoffman, C. J., Aultman, D., & Pipes, P., "A nutrition survey of and recommendations for individuals with Prader-Willi Syndrome who live in group homes", *Journal of the American Dietetic Association, 92*(7), 823-830, 833., 1992.

Johnson, R. K., Goran, M. I., Ferrara, M. S., & Poehlman, E. T., 1995). Athetosis increases resting metabolic rate in adults with cerebral palsy. *Journal of the American Dietetic Association, 96*(2), 145-148.

Murphy, M. D., Ireton-Jones, C. S., Hilman, B. C., Gorman, M. A., & Liepa, G. U., "Resting energy expenditures measured by indirect calorimetry are higher in preadolescent children with cystic fibrosis than expenditures calculated from prediction equations", *Journal of the American Dietetic Association, 95*(1), 30-33, 1995

Sinden, A. A. & Sutphen, J. L., "Dietary treatment of lactose intolerance in infants and children", *Journal of the American Dietetic Association, 91*(12), 1567-1571,1991

Thommessen, M., Riis, G., Kase, B. F., Larsen, S., & Heiberg, A., "Energy and nutrient intakes of disabled children: Do feeding problems make a difference?" *Journal of the American Dietetic Association, 91*(12), 1522-1525, 1991

Unonu, J. N., & Johnson, A. A., "Feeding patterns, food energy, nutrient intakes, and anthropometric measurements of selected black preschool children with Down syndrome", *Journal of the American Dietetic Association, 92*(7), 856-858, 1992

Yadrick, K. & Sneed, J., "Nutrition services for children with developmental disabilities and chronic illnesses in education programs", *Journal of the American Dietetic Association, 94*(10), 1122-1128, 1994

Index

Active management 212
Air-cooled machining 113
Ancillary services 1
Audiovisual (AV) 30
Average Daily Rate (ADR) 129

Behavioral Modifications 110
Box-shaped machines 108

Catering department organization 24
Catering operations 12
Catering service production 3
Chain-of-command policies 23
Coat-checking facilities, 28
Combustion products 43
Commercial dishwashers 108
Commercial refrigeration equipment 221
Communications skills 25
Conceptual Skills 25
Conflict-of-interest dilemmas 33
Contract foodservice operator 10
Control systems 115
Conventional faucets 111
Cross-contamination 213
Customer feedback 96
Customer-contact skills 25

Door-type Machines 108

Electronic Point-of-Sale (EPOS) 94
Ethnic restaurants 81

Fast-food operations 81
Financial capabilities 93
Food safety management 214
Food service operations 108
Foodservice
    facility 113
    functions 6
    operation 1, 10
    operators 97
    programs 11
Fraternal organizations 14
Freestanding restaurant. 81
Full-Service Restaurants 2

Garbage Disposals 113
Geographic Information System (GIS) 120
Gross Profit Percentage (GPP) 97

High-density population 3
Home-replacement food 11
Hotel catering services 7, 10

Ice- making machines, 106, 112
Independent caterers 9
In-house catering 6
Institutional facilities 9
Institutional foodservice 84
Intangible elements 93
Interpersonal Skills 25

Kentucky Fried Chicken (KFC) 121
Kitchen operations 106

Launch Revised Menu Item 105

Management practices 34
Market feasibility study 117
Matrix techniques 90
Mechanical Modifications 110
Menu Retention 100
Microorganisms 107, 225

National Restaurant Association (NRA) 13
Nonprofit organizations 10
Normal management functions 18

Off-premise catering 4
Operational philosophy 114
Organizational structure 21

Plug-in gas connection 39
Pre-rinse Sprayers 112
Profit-and-loss (P&L) 125

Qualitative Approach 92
Quick-service restaurants 81

Recontamination 220
Return on Investment (ROI) 116

Safety arrangements 36
Self-contained facility 10
Standard Operating Procedures (SOPs) 214
Standard specifications 104
Statistical generalization 93
Suburban restaurants 3

Tax-exempt organizations 17
Technical foodservice skills 34
Temperature measurement 213

Uniform System of Accounts 125

Ventilation systems 40

Water-using equipment 106